Medicine
for
the
Earth

Also by Sandra Ingerman

Soul Retrieval: Mending the Fragmented Self
Welcome Home: Following Your Soul's Journey Home
A Fall to Grace

THREE RIVERS PRESS • NEW YORK

Medicine
for
the
Earth

*How to Transform Personal
and Environmental Toxins*

Sandra Ingerman

Grateful acknowledgment is made to:

Story People for permission to reprint an
excerpt from the story "Imagining World" from
Still Mostly True by Brian Andreas, copyright © 1994.

DeVorss Publications for permission to reprint an excerpt from
Law and the Promise by Neville and *Seedtime and Harvest* by Neville.

Published by Three Rivers Press, New York, New York.
Member of the Crown Publishing Group.

Random House, Inc. New York, Toronto, London, Sydney, Auckland
www.randomhouse.com

Three Rivers Press is a registered trademark and the Three Rivers Press colophon
is a trademark of Random House, Inc.

Printed in the United States of America

Design by Lynne Amft

Library of Congress Cataloging-in-Publication Data
Ingerman, Sandra.
Medicine for the earth: how to transform personal and environmental toxins / by Sandra
Ingerman.—1st ed.
Includes bibliographical references.
1. Spiritual healing. 2. Consciousness—Religious aspects. 3. Shamanism. I. Title.
BL65.M4 I44 2001
291.3′1—dc21
00-037431

ISBN 0-609-80517-7

10 9 8 7 6 5 4 3

To Michael Harner and to all the spiritual helpers in my life

And in memory of Katherine Hubbard

and Brooke London Isberg

Contents

Medicine
for
the
Earth

Introduction

In the late 1970s I spent some of my summers in the South Umpqua Valley of Oregon. One year I was a pinecone picker, and another year I was a firefighter for the Forest Service. Every free day I would soak up the sun on a beach along the South Umpqua River. I loved that river; its clarity and beauty touched me in the same way I craved to be touched by life.

As I lay on the beach one day listening to the healing sounds of the rushing river, I began to wonder if there was a way to reverse river pollution. I had graduated from San Francisco State University with a B.A. in biology and had specialized in marine biology, so my thoughts were naturally drawn to the water. Rivers were pure magic to me, and I felt sad knowing that the beauty of so many of the world's rivers were being forever changed by pollution.

These reflections led me to consider returning to school to obtain a master's degree in biology and possibly write a thesis on reversing river pollution. I started contacting schools and soon found a college in Washington whose biology department faculty shared my enthusiasm. As I began to formally apply, I suddenly stopped in my tracks. I didn't really want to be a scientist; I wanted to work with people.

After a great deal of soul searching, I enrolled in the California Institute of Asian Studies (now called the California Institute of Integral Studies) in the counseling psychology program. On Halloween weekend of 1980, destiny led me to take a shamanism course with Dr. Michael Harner, anthropologist and author of *The Way of the Shaman*. I finished my master's-level program in counseling psychology in 1982 with a passion for practicing shamanism instead of traditional counseling.

Shamanism was the first spiritual practice of humankind. Evidence suggests that it dates back at least forty thousand years—some anthropologists would argue that it is more than a hundred thousand years old. Shamans are found in many cultures worldwide, but the word *shaman* comes from the Tungus tribe of Siberia. A shaman is a man or woman who heals the spiritual aspect of illness: diagnosing and treating illnesses, divining information for the community, communicating and interacting with the spirit world, and often acting as a psychopomp, helping souls cross over to the other worlds.

Michael Harner's work with shamanism had led him to explore the common shamanic practices performed in different regions of the world. He found that the practice of shamanism is distinguished by what is called the shamanic journey. Mircea Eliade, author of *Shamanism: Archaic Techniques of Ecstasy,* describes a shaman as a person who journeys in an altered state of consciousness outside time and space.[1] Through these journeys, the shaman retrieves healing help and information for patients, family, friends, and community. Evidence of shamanic journeys is found in Siberia and other parts of Asia, Lapland, Africa, Australia, and native North and South America.

Shamans typically enter an altered state of consciousness through listening to percussion, which allows their soul to take flight to what Carlos Castaneda termed nonordinary reality. Within this reality, shamans travel to three different realms: the Lower World, the Middle World, and the Upper World. The Lower World and the Upper World—which Australian Aborigines call the Dreamtime—Michael Harner considers the "home of the compassionate spirits." In these realms the shaman works with helpful spirits in the form of power animals, known as guardian spirits, and human teachers, who traditionally were religious figures or deceased ancestors.

There are many levels in the Lower World and the Upper World, as we live in an unlimited universe. Through exploration of these nonordinary realms, one can travel to different levels and experience varied landscapes as well as communicate with different power animals and teachers, who will have healing help to offer and great wisdom to share.

The Lower World is reached through a tunnel that leads into the earth. The landscape tends to be earthy, filled with mountains, deserts, seas, dense jungles, and forest. The Upper World is experienced by many as being ethereal. The light tends to be bright, and the colors tend to go from soft pastels to complete darkness. In the Upper World I know I'm standing on something but can't feel the earth below my feet. The landscapes here can be quite varied. I might find myself in a crystal city or just simply in the clouds. The Middle World is the spiritual side of our ordinary world and is used by shamans to find lost and stolen objects and perform long-distance healings.

Since 1980 I have used the shamanic journey as my spiritual practice, to receive guidance for both myself and my clients and for healing spiritual illnesses whose symptoms can manifest as emotional or physical problems. In 1985 I joined the international faculty of the Foundation for Shamanic Studies, directed by Michael Harner. Since then I have taught shamanic journeying and healing practices to thousands of students around the world.

One of the beauties of shamanic journeying is that it allows for direct spiritual revelation. For example, the compassionate spirits have taught me how to live in harmony with nature, how to solve problems, and how to heal myself and others. I can honestly say that I would not be here today if it were not for the love, counsel, and wisdom the spirits have shared with me. Because of this, I am forever grateful to them.

Twenty years of journeying on the question of reversing pollution led me to write this book. The first seed was planted when both the spirits and my intuition told me that ancient people around the world knew how to transmute toxins.

I feverishly began envisioning the chapters. When I told others I was writing a book on transmutation, they were initially caught up in my excitement, but then inevitably asked the same question you may be asking: "What is transmutation?"

The word *transmutation* conjures up many different symbols and images: the old alchemists transmuting base metals into gold, Jesus turning water into wine, Jesus multiplying the loaves and fishes, or Moses parting the Red Sea while the Jews escaped from Egypt. Transmutation, as it is defined in this book, is the ability to transform poisons in the body and in the environment. Ancient texts, especially the Bible, are filled with metaphorical stories referring to this knowledge. Discussed in spiritual traditions worldwide, it is stored somewhere in every person's unconscious, and this book will provide you with several keys to unlock its riches.

Sadly, the art of transmutation has been lost to many modern-day cultures. It vanished when we began to imbue science with the power to "save" us. Despite the lifesaving advances that have been made, many illnesses still have scientists puzzled, and our environment has become increasingly dangerous.

Although in the 1970s great strides were made in cleaning up the rivers, bays, and air, plenty remains to be done. Fish from a rapidly expanding number of waters are considered too dangerous to eat. Corporations still pollute our natural resources, and the ozone layer continues to diminish. Reports on what constitutes proper nutrition change monthly, confusing the public. One study claims a vitamin is good for us, while another says it causes cancer. The FDA now states that it may be dangerous to eat store-bought chicken and meat containing antibiotics, since antibiotic-resistant bacteria may emerge as a result. Now supermarkets have introduced genetically engineered foods without truly knowing what problems these foods may cause.

And, not surprisingly, many of us have lost trust in allopathic medicine to cure ills.

However, I do not wish to focus on the problems. I want us to learn to use our energy to create beauty and healing in our lives and on the planet. I contend that we can reverse environmental pollution through spiritual methods. I do believe that science and the mystical traditions can work together to offer solutions to the world's maladies, but first we must reacquaint ourselves with the knowledge of the great mystics.

The mystical traditions that speak to the ability to transform and transmute poisons are a valuable resource. Their stories of how certain gifted people harmonized with nature to restore health to the environment have much to teach us.

Recently fires burned out of control in the rain forests of South America. Out of desperation, the government called in shamans to make rain. Two days after their arrival, rain came. What resource did these shamans use?

While in the Dutch resistance during World War II, Jack Schwarz was captured by the Gestapo and tortured. But before his torturer's eyes his wounds healed. Later on public TV, he had needles put in him, then healed right in front of the camera. What resource did he use?

People from all over the world have made pilgrimages to places of healing, from Lourdes, France, to the Santuario de Chimayo in New Mexico. Miraculous healings continue to be reported. What resource is at work here?

In *Medicine for the Earth* I will speak to the mystery of these miracles and more. I will weave stories of transmutation given to us by ancient and contemporary mystics and take you step by step through the spiritual practices necessary to access their healing knowledge. I will introduce you to certain changes in consciousness that are essential if we are once again to embrace and use this wisdom.

Let's take a look at some of the alchemists' goals regarding transmutation. In *The Pillar of Celestial Fire* Robert Cox explains:

> The tradition of alchemy has roots in virtually every ancient culture on the planet. The ultimate dream of the alchemist was to produce the Elixir of Life or the Philosopher's Stone. These were believed capable of transmuting the ordinary human body into a perfect, incorruptible, spiritualized body, and of transmuting ordinary metal into a perfect, incorruptible metal—gold.[2]

Manly P. Hall, author of *The Secret Teachings of All Ages,* accumulated an incredible wealth of information about the ancient alchemists. He believed that alchemy was one of the two oldest sciences known to the world. He writes:

> The purpose of alchemy was not to make something out of nothing but rather to fertilize and nurture the seed which was already present. Its processes did not actually create gold but rather made the ever-present seed of gold grow and flourish. Everything which exists has a spirit—the seed of divinity within itself—and regeneration is not the process of attempting to place something where it previously existed. Regeneration actually means the unfoldment of the omnipresent Divinity in man, that this Divinity may shine forth as a sun and illumine all with whom it comes in contact.[3]

Transmutation, as I present it in this book, is learning how to merge with your own divinity to change what the alchemists call heavy leaded consciousness into gold, light consciousness. My intention is to use this ancient knowledge not to teach you how to literally create gold, but to help you bring out your own divinity, thus transmuting your life into a gold that yields greater wealth than the metal would ever bring you. I will teach you the importance of creating the space that allows change to happen instead of trying to make change happen.

Pythagoras urged humankind "to prefer the treasures of the mind and soul to accumulations of earthly goods." In the Golden Verses of Pythagoras he says that if we transcend our lower material nature, we will once again unite with the gods and partake of their immortality.[4]

When I was a child growing up in Brooklyn, the world seemed so magical to me. I loved to sing to the trees, the birds, and the moon, and I heard them sing back. I was greatly influenced by Felix the Cat, who could always reach into his magic bag of tricks for whatever he needed to help him. If you also experienced a magical world as a child, you know how rich your surroundings seemed to you. If you didn't, you can still explore the richness of the magical, invisible realms and engage in the divine dance with all of life.

In *The Unfolding Self,* Ralph Metzner, researcher and teacher in the area of consciousness, defines transmutation in psychological terms. He says alchemy was an early attempt to create a science of consciousness that includes the idea of the transmutation of elements. From a psychological perspective, the elements represent aspects of our nature which can be transmuted from a state of chaos to a state of harmony and balance.[5]

Disharmony causes disease. When we return to a life of balance, healing follows. Living this harmonious existence, we gain a true understanding of the beauty of life. When something is aligned with its own nature as well as the natural world, a state of harmony is created that is then perceived by others as an object of great beauty.

Before we can truly appreciate the beauty we experience outside ourselves and in the earth, we must see and honor our own beauty within. Before we can have harmony outside, we must experience it inside. Therefore we must change ourselves before we can affect our outer world. To do this, it is essential to find our inner light and divinity as well as neutralize or transmute our mental demons through daily spiritual practice so that we gain inner peace. Speaking in metaphor, we must die in order to live. This statement refers to the little deaths we must experience to keep us connected with the divine.

Manly Hall teaches us that hidden in Hermetic philosophy is the true knowledge that we must undergo "an alchemy of the soul" before performing alchemy in the world. We must allow ourselves to be born again to accomplish the Great Work. This is the key to success in performing alchemy, and students will find themselves disappointed in their results if they haven't undergone the personal transformation required to effect change in the outer world.[6] Some form of death occurs in all transformative processes. As we proceed with our work we will see that transmutation requires us to keep letting go of our ego and surrender to the power of the universe and divine forces responsible for miracles.

Paracelsus, born around 1493, is known as one of the most famous alchemical and Hermetic philosophers. He treated and cured leprosy, cholera, and cancer. Paracelsus had a teacher who was an alchemist named Solomon Trismosin. Trismosin reportedly could transmute metals into gold and used his alchemical knowledge to keep himself alive for 150 years. In his work *Alchemical Wanderings*, Manly Hall cites Trismosin, who says we must study who we truly are and our connection with all of life. In doing this, we find that all that we perceive outside ourselves is also within.[7]

I will show that bringing your consciousness into a state of harmony and balance will impact both your own health and the health of the environment. As Ron Roth, who served as a Roman Catholic priest for more than twenty-five years and now teaches modern mysticism and healing through prayer to people of all faiths, so aptly states in *The Healing Path of Prayer*, "According to the spiritual law, as we repair damage on the spiritual level, the natural world begins to be repaired at the same time."[8] This is the true medicine for the earth.

In learning how to change and heal ourselves from the inside out, we must embark on a spiritual path. As a culture, we have lost ourselves in a rational, mechanistic, and scientific reality. Our priorities have become out of balance as gathering material wealth has become important to us. We have forgotten the magic we once knew. African shaman Malidoma Somé describes this phenomenon in *Ritual, Power, Healing, and Community:*

> Indigenous people are indigenous because there are no machines between them and their gods. There are no machines barring the door to the spirit world where one can enter in and listen to what is going on within at a deep level, participating in the vibration of Nature. Where machines speak in place of gods, people are hard put to listen, even more hard put to vibrate with the realm of Nature.[9]

Stories that come from the Bible, from the Kabbalah, and from various Taoist, Hindu, yogic, alchemical, Egyptian, and shamanic works show that miracles were once an everyday occurrence. Miracles still happen today but are not the norm. During one of my journeys I spoke with my spiritual teacher, the Egyptian goddess Isis, who told me that in our current age the spiritual realms are separate from the physical world. In ancient times ordinary reality and the nonordinary realms were not separate. The gods and goddesses roamed the earth, hence the stories of their human and spiritual forms spoken of in Egypt.

But now the veils between the worlds are closed. We are so out of touch with our own beauty and essence that the illusions we believe in are clouding the truth and our reality has become murky. It is time to reopen the curtain and again call the spiritual realms down to earth so that we may more clearly see the perfection in all things. We must once again access both the spiritual realms and divine power to create miraculous healings. As Albert Einstein said, "Mysticality is the power of all true science."

According to Hindu legend, we are living in the time of the Kali

Yuga, a dark age for humankind. I believe this darkness refers to when the veils between the worlds are closed, separating us from the divine and the spiritual realms and therefore separating us from our divinity. Herein lies the "fall from grace." The fall *to* grace will come when we once again link with the spiritual forces that create magic and meaning in our lives. This connection will return to us the harmony necessary to transmute illness in ourselves and our environment.

Many shamans say that we are dreaming the wrong dream. We live with the illusions that we are separate from nature, separate from the spiritual realms, and victims of our life and environment. These illusions are seeds that grow into plants of fear, anger, hate, despair, and darkness. It is time to weed out these plants of illusion from our garden and plant new seeds. As a culture, we have forgotten how to vision, so we have been thrown into the chaos of the universe, manifesting lives based on confused and troubled thoughts. If we have the opportunity to create a different illusion, let's dream a dream that embraces love, harmony, connection to all, and, most important, joy.

William Shakespeare wrote, "All the world's a stage, and all the men and women merely players." It's time for us to wake up to the fact that we are simply acting out roles in this lifetime. It's time to disidentify with these roles and costumes and realize that a bigger picture exists, a grander universe beyond the small, limited world we have created. And it's time to expand our horizons and lift the curtain we have drawn between illusion and truth, so that the spirits, the divine, and our bodies can once again dance together on this earth. We will then return to the golden age that we have lost.

When working with ancient spiritual knowledge, we must remember that such wisdom was often shared through metaphor and allegory. These stories were not meant to be taken literally.

For example, in a journey I was once told that I needed to do more gardening. I took this information at face value, assuming that the spirits were trying to get me out in nature more, because I had become lost in my fast-paced life. However, I was not born with a green thumb, so my gardening attempts were disastrous. Spending more time outside was healing for me, I must admit. After a summer of planting and weeding with not much to show for it, I realized that the spirits were not suggesting that I literally go out and plant a garden. They were suggesting that I see and work with life as a garden. They were asking me to use the metaphors of gardening when I saw clients and taught shamanism workshops.

When doing spiritual healing work, it is very easy to plant seeds of fear in a client by sharing a negative prophecy. But as people who already live lives so full of fear, we need not more of the same, but rather inspiration to heal. The spirits were trying to teach me to introduce seeds of love and hope instead of seeds of fear.

Once I realized the true meaning of the spirits' message, my work with people and my teaching changed to incorporate this healing knowledge. I began to practice using seed words that would grow into plants of love, hope, and inspiration instead of plants of fear.

One of my students once asked me to help work with one of her clients who had cancer. The woman went on a shamanic journey in which she presented her helping spirit with the question "Am I going to die?" The helping spirit she went to responded, "Yes." However, my interpretation of this response was less literal: If a person is dealing with a life-threatening illness, she must die in order to live. The process of healing a major illness puts a person through so many changes that it often seems as if a death has occurred—and it has.

The compassionate spirits, who intend to further our growth and expansion, would not blurt out information about a person's physical death. There is only one road to walk down with such literal information, in addition, we miss the truth of the wisdom being shared. But when concepts are presented metaphorically, we are forced to open to a different depth of wisdom and grow on other levels.

Through metaphorical stories, legends, and allegories, the mystics teach us how to use the power of transmutation to heal ourselves and the environment. They teach us that transmutation is about placing our feet on the ground, putting our hands up to the sky, and playing with the forces of nature as well as the power of the universe. St. Germain describes this so well when he says:

> Thus alchemy, when properly understood, deals with the conscious power of controlling mutations and transmutations within Matter and energy and even within life itself. It is the science of the mystic and it is the forte of the self-realized man who, having sought, has found himself to be one with God and is willing to play his part.[10]

After a friend of mine read the manuscript version of *Medicine for the Earth,* she commented that as the old formulas we have been living by drop away, this book gives people a new formula to gracefully fall into. In order to reintroduce or unlock this ancient wisdom, it is essential that we begin by incorporating spiritual practices into our life. We first need to catch up to the state of consciousness the mystics attained before we can perform the miracles they have accomplished.

After reading the vast range of stories of the miracle of transmutation, I analyzed the elements they all shared. A formula naturally emerged: intention + love + harmony + union + focus + concentration + imagination = transmutation.

This formula is a gestalt, a hologram whose components all work together and are inseparable from the whole. This is not a linear formula. Thus I have organized the book so that each part will help you tap into your unconscious and access the powers of each element—intention, love, harmony, union, focus, concentration, and imagination. In this way, you will ultimately understand the path to transmutation through your own practice.

The transmutation formula appears at various places in the book where needed to help connect the preceding material with our work in transmutation or to help you process what you are learning. Each time I present the formula for transmutation, I will summarize how the material relates to healing the earth.

The dance I will take you through begins with Part I, "Creation and Union," which teaches you how to access the divine power that will work with you to perform transmutation. Union is a wonderful experience, but modern life provides many daily stresses, and our strong egos distract us from our spiritual path. Part II, "Separation Versus Union," gives a variety of tools necessary to help you reconnect with the divine principle when you get lost in the egoic problems of life. Part III, "Love and Imagination," teaches how to create a sacred space that welcomes spirit's presence and how to use imagination as a creative force in your own and others' lives. Part IV, "Harmony with Nature Within and Without," discusses how reconnecting with nature harmonizes us with both ourselves and all of life. From this harmonious state, transmutation will naturally flow.

Next I share with you specific practices that have been used throughout the world to call down the divine. Part V, "Transmutation," will specifically describe the acts that must be performed for transmutation to occur. In Part VI, "Ceremonies for Transmutation," I will instruct you on the use and creation of ceremonies, then suggest ceremonies that you can use to begin to work with the power of transmutation. In the Epilogue, I will share the first transmutation experiments I performed with groups in which we worked with chemically polluted water. I will discuss the preparation work we did, the ceremony used, the results of our work, what we learned, and how we felt changed from the work.

If you have read any of my previous books—*Soul Retrieval, Welcome Home,* and *A Fall to Grace*—you might notice that some concepts have been repeated in *Medicine for the Earth,* These concepts are building blocks essential to our exploration of transmutation and here assume a different meaning that will take you deeper within your work.

You will notice that I repeat certain statements throughout the book. This was an intentional choice on my part as certain principles are so key to the success of transmutation that I wanted to imbed them in your consciousness.

Each section of the book offers exercises to help you work with the material directly. It is important to do the exercises, because the ideas in this book cannot be used solely as mental constructs. You must become and live what is written here. Also, this book will not teach you magic. The "magic" of transmutation comes from learning to love yourself and all of life. Once you raise your consciousness and awareness, it will lead you to take action in your life. This process requires devotion and commitment to daily spiritual practice; there are no shortcuts.

People often become attracted to spiritual paths because they imagine they will gain certain results. However, when they discover the depth of commitment required to walk down this road, they often get off it, looking for an easier trail. All spiritual paths require daily commitment. You can search for a short and easy road, but let me save you some time and energy: It doesn't exist.

The other trap people sometimes get caught in is trying to use the rational mind to understand and dissect the mysteries of life instead of doing the work. Caroline Casey, astrologer and author, shares a Haitian proverb that says, "The gods won't appear, the magic won't happen, if we are not living our real life. Studying life is not living life, and therefore has no magic."[11]

Reading and working with the material in *Medicine for the Earth* is like being part of an adventure to hunt for hidden treasure. You will find that Parts I and II are the preparation for a great adventure. Some of you will find yourself excited and stimulated by the mapping work needed to be accomplished before the great adventure can begin. Some of you will feel like saying, "Let's get on with it." Please remember that the Great Work cannot be achieved without the work of transforming ourselves first. Don't give up on discovering great treasure because you didn't want to walk down the path to get there.

I recommend that you read all of *Medicine for the Earth* before doing the exercises. In this way, you will see the path I am leading you down and can decide if you wish to walk it. The exercises given are ones that I have found helpful in working with myself and others. However, you are a creative genius in your own right. If you imagine something different, follow your own creative process.

If you are trained in shamanic journeying or another system of accessing spiritual information, use the system you know to do these exercises. If you are new to receiving personal spiritual revelation, follow the exercises' instructions, which will place you in a meditative state. If you find yourself having a hard time connecting with your inner knowing and truth, you may wish to seek out a workshop on a spiritual system you feel drawn to, and learn how to access your own guidance.

You may also want to start a journal in which you describe the answers you receive from some of the exercises, or you might jot down words as answers in the margin. Do what keeps you engaged in the process in whatever way best fits your nature.

Go slow with your process; this work is deep and powerful. We can learn from a Hindu legend about the god Shiva. Although Shiva was sure he could transmute the poisons of the world, he was not truly ready. When he swallowed them, they became stuck in his throat, and he turned blue. Take your time, and each day that you work, your life will change in beautiful ways.

We tend to lead our lives at a pretty frantic pace. It's important to acknowledge that the power of the mysteries comes through deep contemplation, not through learning techniques. We gain wisdom from remembering, and remembering comes from sitting. Sitting inside yourself and within nature will awaken your dormant intuitive knowing about what is important in life, as well as truths you may have forgotten. Make healing yourself and the environment a priority. Give yourself the time you need to sink into what you are learning. In this way, when the time for transmutation begins, you will not turn blue, but move toward divine light.

One of the causes of illness in our culture today is isolation. The fact that we no longer live and work cooperatively within our community creates a loneliness that can lead to emotional and physical illness. We can become overwhelmed by how much needs to be done in our environment when there seems to be no one to share the burden with. Working in community can be very healing on many levels. Thus you may choose to form a group of like-minded individuals to cover the material presented in *Medicine for the Earth*. If you do work in a group, remember not to get caught up in who is right or who is getting "better" answers. Enjoying a community means sharing all the pieces of the puzzle, which will begin to come together if you honor each person's offerings.

I have spent years journeying on the subject of transmutation and reading texts from the world's spiritual traditions. Some of the books I have read are quite old, while others are more modern. Some are steeped in metaphor and allegory, to keep us from uncovering secrets before we are ready. But I can summarize all that I have learned in a few lines:

> *All life is of the light*
> *I am light*
> *We are light*
> *Turn everything into light*

So let's begin.

I

Creation and Union

Imagine yourself sitting in a quiet place in nature, being still and silent inside yourself.

Breathe in the power of the universe.

Breathe out the power of universe.

Breathe in the love of the divine.

Breathe out the love of the divine.

Breathe in the light of the Absolute.

Breathe out the light of the Absolute.

As you inspire the power, love, and light of the universe, you exhale sharing love and light with all living beings. As you breathe, experience yourself expanding into the eternal light of all life. You are not a separate entity, you are one with all that is.

Imagine.

The Creation Myth

Give light and the darkness will disappear of itself.
— ERASMUS

When looking at miracle stories of healing, the key element involved in transmutation of energy is the ability to move out of an egoic state of consciousness, where one feels separate from the rest of life, into a state of union with the power of the universe or the creator.

The Bible relates many stories of miraculous healings performed by Jesus in union with the creator. In *The Healing Path of Prayer* Ron Roth emphasizes how Bible passages about prayer for healing have been distorted by translation and how important it is to connect with the energy of the universe when transmuting energy for healing. Roth contends that when Jesus's words were translated from the Aramaic, much of what he was truly trying to communicate was lost. One example of this is where Jesus told his disciples to pray and to heal in his name. To understand the true meaning of this, one must have the same understanding of the essence of God's nature that Jesus had, as well as the same concept of creation and oneness with it. In performing the miracle of transmutation as Jesus did, one must move into a state of union with the creator rather than petition Jesus for help.[1]

Some modern-day mystics have similar views on the nature of healing. Jack Schwarz, as mentioned in the introduction, is a remarkable man who has always had the power to heal himself. During

World War II he terrorized his Nazi torturers by healing his wounds in their presence. He writes in *How to Master the Art of Personal Healing* how under laboratory conditions he healed his wounds when he had long sailmaker's needles put through his body. Sometimes the needles were contaminated with viruses or bacteria. In all cases he had no pain, bleeding, or infection.[2]

Schwarz says that he heals himself through heightened consciousness and attuning to the universe. He believes that it is our potential that the Scriptures refer to when talking about God and omnipotence. He tells us we all have the same ability for attaining such consciousness and healing as he did; we just need to believe in ourselves.[3]

Sai Baba is a contemporary mystic who has demonstrated miraculous manifestations and healings to thousands of people. A client of mine who had been in the audience of Sai Baba at his ashram in India told me of a miraculous feat he performed. Amongst ten thousand people at the ashram, he walked up to her, put a ring in her hand, and said, "You have been looking for this, haven't you?" It was her wedding ring, which she had lost down a sink drain years before.

Like Schwarz, Sai Baba also emphasizes our potential for such higher consciousness by saying: "That he is God, that we also are God, and that the only difference between him and ourselves is that he is ever aware of, and lives fully in his truth, whereas we are unaware of our truth."[4]

Stories about miracles are based on the ability to merge with a higher power. To transmute energy one must be in harmony and union with the source of life. However, in our world today, technology has separated us from natural forces, and most of us lack the spiritual foundation necessary to answer the following questions:

Be in harmony with what?
Be in union with what?
Have faith in what?
Trust in what?

We need to remember that we are more than our egoic self, and we must expand our state of consciousness, embracing and merging with a higher power, whether the higher power is called God, source, the light, the absolute, the power of the universe, the unnameable, the unknowable, the all-knowing, the web of life, the spirit that lives in all things, the great goddess, Jesus, Buddha, Allah, Kuan Yin, Kali, Mary, Tara, Wankan Tanka, White Buffalo Woman, or any other name.

In our culture, we often get stuck in our family history and the illusion that we are our families and take our creation only back to our immediate ancestors. This has its place, as we shall see later on. But to merge and be in union with the creator, we must remember the source from which we ultimately came.

To address the issue of our creation, it is helpful to look at creation myths, which all cultures possess. The creation myth is the essential building block for the spiritual foundation we work with. The cross-cultural study of creation myths is fascinating and enlightening for our own understanding of source. Metaphorical stories shape cultural beliefs as well as morals.

In *Primal Myths,* a book on creation myths from around the world, Barbara Sproul, director of the Program in Religion at Hunter College in New York, states that an important function of myths is to reveal abstract universal truths through stories told "in the familiar world of time and space" and which contain common details.[5]

Today no one creation story reflects the diverse population of our communities, which are made up of people of different races, religions, and philosophical beliefs. Since we live in increasingly multicultural communities, it is more and more important to understand the myths of various cultures. It is helpful to incorporate your own words and spiritual beliefs into a personal creation myth that will function as your doorway to understanding the unity all ancient and modern mystics speak of. For this reason we will look at some examples of creation myths, and then I will lead you down the road to develop your own.

In our society, perhaps the best-known creation myth is that related in the first book of Genesis:

> In the beginning God created the heavens and the earth. The earth was without form and void, and darkness was upon the face of the deep; and the Spirit of God was moving over the face of the waters.
>
> And God said, "Let there be light"; and there was light. And God saw that the light was good; and God separated the light from the darkness. God called the light Day, and the darkness he called Night. And there was evening and there was morning, one day.
>
> And God said, "Let there be a firmament in the midst of the waters, and let it separate the waters from the waters." And God made the firmament and separated the waters which were under the firmament from the waters which were above the firmament. And it was so. And God called the firmament Heaven. And there was evening and there was morning, a second day.
>
> And God said, "Let the waters under the heavens be gathered together into one place, and let the dry land appear." And it was so. God called the dry land Earth, and the waters that were gathered together he called Seas. And God saw that it was good. And God said, "Let the earth put forth vegetation, plants yielding seeds bearing fruit in which is their seed, each according to its kind, upon the earth. And it was so. The earth brought forth vegetation, plants yielding seed according to their own kinds, and trees bearing fruit in which is their seed, each according to its kind. And God saw that it was good. And there was evening and there was morning, a third day. (Genesis 1:1–13)

The creation story of Genesis continues with God creating the light in a way that distinguished days, seasons, and years. Then he created the birds, sea creatures, and the rest of the animal and plant kingdoms. He finished his work by creating man in his own image. Through his power of creation he gifted all living beings with food. And on the seventh day, satisfied with what he created, God rested.

Metaphoric and symbolic expression, the language of myths, are of great importance in spiritual teachings, since they can often be used to make otherwise obtuse but significant principles comprehensible. As we begin to look at writing our own story of creation we will look more into using symbolic representations.

In *Primal Myths* Barbara Sproul describes how myths reflect values and the power of metaphors to express them. She says we can misinterpret myths by confusing myth and science. Sproul uses Genesis as an example of this, raising the question of whether God created the universe in literally six days or whether the Hebrew authors used this as a symbolic time frame. She believes that when we tie myths to fact and literal interpretation, we miss the point. Myth teaches values and meaning. Metaphor is a necessary component to understanding how the absolute creates. In working with myth, it's important not to pit a creation story against science and facts, but to see myth as a metaphorical story of your beliefs.[6]

As you think about what you have read, watch your reactions to Genesis and to what Barbara Sproul says about metaphor and not creating an opposition between science and stories of creation. You want to begin to incorporate your own beliefs into a story of creation. For you cannot merge or have union with the creator unless your story truly speaks to your soul.

To understand the miracles Jesus performed as reported in the Bible, and to begin envisioning what the creator looks like to you, it is important to understand the force he merged with to accomplish his healings.

In my life I have had a few brushes with death and experienced classic near-death experiences (NDEs) during these times. I did have the experience of going to God. My experience of God is that God is not male or female. God to me is pure light—a light that cannot compare to any light I have seen. God to me is pure love—a kind of love I will probably not experience on this earthly plane. I was not judged for who I was; to God, I was just pure essence and light. For me the notion that God created man in his own image means that God is light and I am also pure light, pure essence.

In *The Healing Path of Prayer* Ron Roth writes that the Aramaic word for God is *Alaha,* from which were derived the Arabic *Allah* and the Hebrew *Elohim.* Roth says that *Alaha* means "essence" or "substance of all being," as well as "breath" or "life force." He says the purpose of prayer is to create, maintain, and nurture a relationship with God and the divine rather than to ask for something. With prayer comes the awareness that with each breath we breathe the divine into ourselves.[7] Using prayer in this way is a beautiful and potent way of staying connected to and merging with the creator, the divine presence in our lives.

Roth also defines God in terms of light and energy. In Genesis God creates form out of formlessness when he decrees, "Let there be light." By creating light first, God brought into being the essence of life, which is light and energy, creating life in his own image.[8]

We will explore the cross-cultural significance of the metaphor of light involved in transcendental experiences and its place in our work with transmutation in Part V.

To add other possible dimensions to a definition of God, consider the following Egyptian story of creation as told by Jean Houston, author and lecturer on myth, history, and psychology, in *The Passion of Isis and Osiris,* and by Normandi Ellis, who teaches writing and has studied Egyptian language and literature for years, in *Awakening Osiris: The Egyptian Book of the Dead.* Houston compares the Egyptian creation myth to Genesis, as they both begin with the spoken word. But for the Egyptians, God was lonely and wanted companionship, so he created life on earth and the gods in heaven—which in actuality were just aspects of himself. The Egyptians were a matriarchal culture, speaking about Mother Sky and Father Earth, and marked time in twenty-eight-day lunar cycles.[9]

Here in part is Houston's account of the Egyptian story of creation:

> In the beginning there was the Great He/She: Atum. Complete. Whole. Perfect. And lonely. Passion without form. Atum was everything and nothing—an ourobouric serpent biting its tail, a cosmic dervish (atom/Atum) whirring in the void, or perhaps nothing more than Spirit. There was neither height nor depth, neither past nor future. All was eternal darkness. A hot breath, a long sigh, moved across the primordial waters of Chaos. Lonely and isolated in His/Her perfection, the divine being desired companionship with an Other, with the possibilities of selves that existed within the one Self. Therefore, the Word was spoken, a breathing of the vowels of a divine name: Atum or Om or Yod-He-Vav-He—all the single name of the Self.

The story continues when Atum, out of the need for companionship, created the gods of magic (Heka), wisdom (Hu), knowledge (Sia), and truth (Ma'at). Atum declared that what the heart desires, combined with the will, "form the Word that becomes the Great Becoming."

Atum knew that he/she was the source of its own self. And out of this union with self Atum begat two children—Shu, the son, the mind, who became the god of air, and Tefnut, the daughter, the passionate and emotional goddess of moisture. In turn, Shu and Tefnut, through their union, gave birth to a daughter, Nut, who became the beautiful body of heaven, and a son, Geb, who became the "passionate life force of Earth." Nut and Geb lay in passionate embrace with each other through eternity as Nut bent over and covered the earth with shimmering stars and Geb rose up to his wife as a hill and a mountain.

Through their love, the love of earth and heaven for each other, emerged the stars and planets, who gave light to the darkened heavens. Nut bore Geb a pair of sons: Ra, the sun, and Thoth, the moon. Sun and moon cycles were birthed, creating time and giving forth the energy for other children to be born, and in this way creation continued.[10]

Normandi Ellis stresses the power of language in creation and the many aspects of Egyptian gods:

> Language was of primary importance; in essence it cast a type of spell. The ancient Egyptians felt that if words could be uttered precisely, in proper sequence and with proper intonation, those words could produce magical effects. The Fourth Gospel begins: In the beginning was the Word. In like manner the Egyptian History of the Creation of the Gods and the World begins with the words of Temu:
>
> *I am he came into being, being what I created—*
> *the creator of the creations . . .*
> *After I created my own becoming,*
> *I created many things*
> *that came forth from my mouth*
>
> In addition, re-a for the mouth and Re (or Ra) for the sun god are similar. The implication, then, may be that Temu opened his mouth and light burst forth. The lions of yesterday and today (time) were symbols of Ra and these were called re-re, or the sound of lions roaring. One begins to see how intricately linked are the sound, symbol, myth and meaning. Language, then, resonates on and on in an intricate spiral of meanings, one word or association leading to the next.

Although there is an abundance of gods and goddesses named in the text, Ellis believes there was a time where the gods were one, the multitudinous gods and goddesses being different aspects of the one god. She goes on to say that the Egyptian word for "god" is *neter.* When applied to Egyptian religion, the English word *god* does not quite fit, as *neter* refers to a spiritual essence or principle. Ellis says, "Our word 'nature' might derive from it through the Latin." Therefore, it is uncertain whether the *neters* were representing gods or the multitudinous natures of one supreme being.[11]

In my own life and work, I incorporate both the concepts of a supreme being and intermediaries as seen in the Egyptian creation myth. As a religious person, I believe in a source of all life represented as an essence of light or as divine love—which is connected to my practice of shamanism.

In shamanism the belief is that we all have helping spirits to whom we can go for the purpose of divining information and for healing. Michael Harner calls these the "compassionate spirits." Taking the form of animals and humans, they are intermediaries who help us with our own life, healing, and spiritual practice.

For example, when I need assistance in answering a question for myself or for a client, I go to my helping spirits for guidance and advice. For me the light I view as a supreme being is not an essence that speaks to me—it has no personality and does not see me as a personality. By contrast, my helping spirits have personalities and essences I can relate to. For example, I have an important connection with a spiritual teacher who takes on the form of the Egyptian goddess Isis, bringing the divine feminine into my life.

In shamanism, we do not use our own energy in doing healing work; we work in partnership with the spirits. The shaman is the hands and heart that the spirits work through. Thus when I am doing shamanic healing work such as restoring lost power, returning lost soul parts, or removing intruding spiritual energy, I merge with my helping spirits. The helping spirits or the compassionate spirits are the conduits of the power of the universe. In merging with the helping spirits, an expansion of consciousness is necessary, since the ego must stand aside for this union to take place. I will explain this in more detail in Part II.

Another way I work with a client is through the laying on of hands. When using this method I seek union with the light, divine love. Thus in direct healing I sometimes choose not to work with intermediaries—although they have the same power to heal—and instead expand my consciousness even more to bring source through to a client, with the aim of creating a spark to light source inside himself.

I employ whatever method I am guided to use for each client. The key to the success of the healing is not whether I go straight to source or whether I use an intermediary, but how successful I am at eliminating my egoistic concerns. I must be in union with a higher power. Egos don't heal; divine love does.

Normandi Ellis also spoke of the multitudinous nature of the supreme being. In the Egyptian creation myth we see a god or goddess for each of the elements—air, earth, fire, and water. There is also a god or spiritual essence of the sun and moon. We know that indigenous people believe that there is a spirit that lives in all things. However, as cultures have become more scientific and rational, we have stopped believing in the invisible worlds and validate only what can be seen with the visible eye. As a result, we have lost our connection with nature and other living beings—what Native Americans call the web of life. In looking at how our dissociation from the web of life has caused personal and environmental illness, we will see how reconnecting with it is part of being able to transmute illness.

When discussing healing work through transmutation of energy, I will use both the words *spirit* and *spirits* to refer to the power with which we must connect. This is because of people's different philosophical beliefs; some people feel more comfortable working with one divine source or spirit, while others may prefer working with many helping spirits, or gods and goddesses, or a combination of both, as I do.

In preparation for envisioning a personal creation myth, it will be instructive to look at the spiritual forces in an adaptation of another creation myth, this time from Australia.

The goddess of the sun, Yhi, brought light into the darkness. The earth, created by Baiame, needed light and warmth in order for life to grow and be nurtured.

Baiame was the all-father who in the beginning of the Dreamtime was life itself. Baiame was thought and intelligence without a body, and was part of his creation, living in every single animal and other life form. He was indivisible and complete.

Baiame decided it was time to show himself to the beings he had created. He shared with Yhi his plans, which were to clothe himself in flesh. From the processes of thought joining together atoms and dust, forming blood, sinew, cartilage, and flesh, he formed an animal that walked erect on two legs. Man was now created as a vessel for the mind-power of the great spirit. Man had hands to make tools as well as the knowledge of how to use them. Man had a brain that could obey the impulse of the spirit.

The spirit of the all-father, happy with his creation, returned to his home in the sky, leaving behind him the crown of his creation, man.[12]

Although you can learn much from looking at the creation myths of other cultures, to have union with a higher power, you must be able to relate to the qualities and appearance of your creator, since it is not possible for you to merge with a higher power you cannot relate to. This applies to any religious precepts forced on us in childhood. Such beliefs will not empower you; it is necessary to claim and honor your own philosophical beliefs here. Moreover, in today's world, where many people get lost in the male dynamic power of the divine, it is time again to balance the male aspect of the divine with the honor accorded to the receptive power of the feminine. This is something you might wish to stress in your creation myth.

As an example of a modern creation myth the following is a story I wrote to express my own sense of the divine:

> Before there was a beginning, there was no time, no thought, nothingness. There was only gray. Out of the grayness grew an expanse of darkness named the void.
>
> The void was empty but yet full. The void was pregnant with endless possibilities. The void was the space where everything to be born was created from. The void was the beginning.
>
> Out of the void grew a great light. This light, which was intelligence, knew of no separation. As there was no separation, there was no state of loneliness. The light was pure love. The light was divine love.
>
> The light had a thought: What would it be like to manifest a being in my image—a being who could learn about manifesting physical form as a spirit? This thought had great power, as all thoughts create physical manifestation. There is no thought that does not manifest itself in physical form.
>
> Out of thought came the word. The word had great magical power. As the word was spoken, the act was done. Earth was created as a playground for spirit to learn how to manifest. The light manifested sky, earth, air, water, and fire to support its manifestations. Animals, insects, rocks, trees, plants, and humankind were created. Humankind was created as an experiment. Humans were given bodies to play in, but also minds that could think and develop and evolve. But it is important to remember that the light created humankind in its own image. So humankind was really light surrounded by this body, which could interact with its development.
>
> The light truly loved all of its creations. All the creations were different manifestations of the light, but were the light itself.
>
> The light gave humans a great gift. Here was the opportunity for spirit to have a body. This body could taste, smell, and feel sen-

sations as well as emotions. This body could know the joys of life on earth.

The creator made the sun, which was the source of life. All life is of the light. All life is nurtured by the light. The sun feeds all the plants, trees, and animals with nutrients. All life pulls light force from the sky and nutrients from the earth. As all life eats and receives gratefully the gifts of the creator, the light sings in joy that life appreciates all that is given by the creation of earth. The light of the moon was created to teach all life about the ebb and flow of nature.

The light created humankind to dance, sing, eat, make love, know love, know the joy of being a spirit in a body. The light created humankind to learn about the adventure of creating thought into physical form. The light created humankind to play. The light created humankind in its own image—light filled with divine love, divine love in a body that can manifest endless possibilities. To know how to go back to the void, the place of endless possibilities, before all creation began to manifest thought into physical reality; to learn to play and love unconditionally while being in a body—this was the purpose of the light creating humankind. And the light said: "May the joyful earth dance begin." And it was done.

For me the creator has no gender and is pure light and divine love. When I merge with the creator, I am in union with a pure essence of light and love.

Now that we have examples of specific creation myths, it is time to write your own. Many people fear the creator because of the influence of the organized religions, which teach us that God is a punishing God. In my near death experiences I only felt the deep unconditional love and accepting presence of God. The work for you here is to get in touch with the love, acceptance, and gentleness of your creator. Imagine what this would look like and feel like to you.

The first step in making your own creation myth is to write a story that you can work with on a deeper level. In many cross-cultural myths, creation began with an absolute power saying a word. The power of word to affect creation was well understood in all cultures. As this is such a significant key to creation and transmutation, we will delve into this work in Part V, after you have built the spiritual foundation necessary to continue. For now, in creating your myth, do not rely too much on your logical, rational mind. Instead relax and put on some music that helps you move into an expanded state of consciousness. Make sure you are wearing comfortable clothes. You might wish to disconnect your phone. Get paper to write with, or go to your computer. Instead of trying to devise a story, let one come. Allow your hands to gently move with your pen or on your computer. See what comes when you just let your hands move over the page or keyboard without thinking. In some teachings this is called automatic writing, where you are letting your unconscious reveal your deep beliefs about your creation instead of trying to force your left brain, your thinking brain, to make something up. Allow the process to happen. Take your time. If you do not get results one day, trust that your psyche will reveal the information to you when you are ready.

Questions you may want to consider before writing your story are:

What do you believe in?
Does your creator have a name?
What does your creator look like?
Does your creator have a gender?
How did creation begin?
Why did your creator decide to create humankind?
What other life forms did your creator make?
What natural elements did your creator make to support life
    forms?

How does your creator take care and nurture his/her life forms?
What qualities are associated with your creator?

The answers to these questions could constitute elements in your story. You might find yourself changing your creation myth as you evolve, aligning it with the higher consciousness you have attained. Remember: To have union with the power of the universe, you must believe in a force to merge with.

Once you have composed your story, you can further develop your ideas by drawing or painting it. Whether your painting is realistic or abstract doesn't matter; it will allow you to connect with the material on a deeper level.

2

Tools to Embody Your Creation Story

The next phase of the process is to work with the power of symbol. You want to devise a symbol for your creation story. The author Dion Fortune in 1919 was initiated into the Hermetic Order of the Golden Dawn, where she studied magic, blending this knowledge with her understanding of psychology. In *The Mystical Qabalah* Fortune explains the necessity of using symbols when expressing abstract concepts such as spiritual ideas. She says that process rather than thought is how we obtain knowledge of higher forms of existence. In communicating transcendental ideas, mystics and philosophers have used "every imaginable simile" as well as a "maze of words" to convey their impressions. But these means have failed to reveal the truth of their realizations.

The Kabbalists successfully use symbols to meditate on, rather than trying to explain to the mind incomprehensible ideas. Fortune says, "The mind can no more grasp the transcendent philosophy than the eye can see music."[1]

In *Primal Myths*, Barbara Sproul reiterates that the vehicle for the expression of myth is symbol. As myths speak to the transcendent and unknowable aspects of life and creation, symbols are used to express their truths.[2]

Sai Baba teaches the importance of allowing the mind to create its own form of the divine versus taking an image of a statue or a picture. This helps us become in union with the creator. Baba tells us, "When the mind creates God's form, then the mind itself becomes that form, and God Himself will fill that form of Himself with His Divinity."[3]

In *Myth, Religion, and Mother Right,* J. J. Bachofen says:

> The symbol awakens intimations; speech can only explain. The symbol plucks all the strings of the human spirit at once; speech is compelled to take up a single thought at a time. The symbol strikes its roots in the most secret depths of the soul; language skims over the surface of the understanding.[4]

Besides using symbols to connect with your unconscious, symbols will also help you merge with a higher power. When you begin to image your creator, if you see him or her as a person, this being will have a physical boundary. Since you also have a boundary created by your body, it's difficult to experience complete union with your creator. You are attempting to get to a place of essence merging with essence. Thus it is beneficial to find a symbol for your essence that can express union with the symbol of your creator's essence.

○ E X E R C I S E S

When you understand the power of symbol, let a symbol of your creator that you can use for meditation form in your mind's eye. This will allow your own unconscious to begin merging with your higher power.

You might wish to draw your symbol and place it somewhere in your house or office where you will see it often. The great psychologist, Carl Jung said that symbols speak to our unconscious. When you see a symbol on a regular basis, it begins to create change in your psyche and your awareness. I have painted a picture of the light I perceive God to be. It sits on the wall in my office where I can see it as I work.

When I get lost in the limitations of my beliefs and attitudes, this symbol reminds me of the power my being truly embraces and the force behind me.

Your next task is to physically embody your creation myth. You cannot experience union with your higher power just by thinking about it. You must truly feel union throughout your entire body.

What I have learned from my own spiritual studies, especially my practice with shamanism, is the power of song and dance. Singing and dancing are used by shamans to help them move their egos out of the way so that the power of the universe can come through. Singing transforms consciousness.

Robert Gass, a lecturer and workshop leader, has been involved with the study of chanting and spiritual music for over twenty years. In *Chanting* he describes another benefit of singing: Through the repetitive sounds of a chant vibrating in our brains, we begin to shift into a more aligned, harmonious state.[5]

Scientific research has revealed that music has a powerful effect, partly because certain sounds have the ability to change the frequency of our brain waves. When we are in an ordinary state of consciousness, our brain waves are in a beta state, a state in which the ego thrives. However, some music can slow down our brain waves, putting us into an alpha or theta state, deep meditative states of consciousness. The theta state is where consciousness can expand our experience of union.

Shamans around the world use percussion to access such an expanded state of consciousness. Many other musical compositions have also been found to slow the brain waves to an alpha or theta state, such as some of the music composed by Mozart and Pachelbel. Shamans also work with power songs, special songs sung only when a shaman is preparing to perform serious spiritual work. Moreover, shamans have different songs for various kinds of healing and divination work.

When a client comes to see me for shamanic healing, I begin by discussing the problem my client is experiencing. Although initially my psychotherapist self comes up with theories about what must have happened in my client's past to cause this problem, I remind myself that from the perspective of a spiritual healer, what my mind thinks about the issue is not important. What matters is what my helping spirits think and how they are going to share the healing energy of the universe with my client. I might also find myself feeling a bit of performance anxiety: Will I be able to contact my helping spirits? Will they really come through?

All of this mind chatter signifies my disconnection with source. Part of the human condition is to have an ego. I believe that the ego was actually created to give us spiritual beings a way to perceive time and space. For without an ego that perceives separation from everything else, how would we know the space we are occupying in the world? But somehow during evolution the ego stopped perceiving itself as a vehicle and came to conceive of itself as running the show.

The question, then, is this: When doing spiritual work, how do we quiet the egoic part of ourselves so that we can allow a greater power to work through us? The metaphor of the shaman being a "hollow bone" describes the state we must achieve to allow the power of the universe to come through us. In this state, the ego steps aside, allowing spiritual power to fill up the shaman.

Have you ever sung in the shower? When you really belt out a song when nobody is listening, you feel as if you have become huge, your energy takes up a greater space than you are used to, and you feel as though nothing can stop you now. I know you have had this experience at least once in your life.

This is what happens when you sing a power song. By really allowing yourself to move into the song, your energy expands and you allow the power of spirit to interact with you.

Before I do any spiritual healing work with a client, I sing my power song for about twenty minutes, until I am no longer experiencing mental chatter, my energy feels so expansive I can't imagine any building that could contain it, and I am in a state of egoless divine love. Some shamans burst into tears as they sing, because of the love that is coursing through their heart.

In my workshops on shamanic journeying, I teach participants to get in touch with their own power songs to facilitate union with the power of the universe. As a psychotherapist, my interest in shamanism has been how to utilize these ancient methods to solve the problems of our time. When I began teaching shamanism in the early 1980s, I was curious about how participants were using in their lives the techniques I had taught them. I asked people to write to me after the workshop and tell me in what ways they might be using shamanic techniques in their everyday lives.

Among the letters I received were some from lawyers who reported that before a difficult court case they would go into a rest room and sing their power song. They were convinced that doing this influenced the court proceedings in their client's favor.

What was really happening in these cases was that when the lawyers sang their power songs, they moved their own egos out of the way so that spirit could come through to empower them and change the course of events. They were having a union experience. Singing dissolves the veil between the worlds, allowing the healing energy of spirit or the spirits to touch us and come through us.

Another spiritual system in which the power of sound is used is that of people from India. They employ mantras for meditation and healing as they invoke higher consciousness.

> Sound is a form of energy made up of vibrations or wavelengths—certain wavelengths have the power to heal, others are capable of shattering glass. Mantras are Sanskrit syllables, words or phrases which, when repeated in meditation, will bring an individual to a higher state of consciousness. They are sounds or energies that have always existed in the universe and can neither be created or destroyed.[6]

In *Chanting* Robert Gass explains that as we chant we begin to breathe more deeply, more slowly, and more rhythmically, producing a state of spiritual and physical well-being. The resonance in our bodies created by chanting makes us feel as if we are being massaged from the inside out. Adding to this, our brain waves are measurably altered, evoking a state of relaxation as well as a state of heightened creativity. Our muscle tension dissipates, and our blood pressure and heart rate decrease.

From the perspective of Eastern thought, chanting is a vehicle for freeing up the vital energy infusing every system, organ, and cell, whether it is called *chi, prana,* or *kundalini.* Therefore, a regular practice of chanting creates a state of health and well-being concept that has long been recognized in other societies and systems of healing.[7]

I often teach workshops in Europe. I noticed for years that when I taught in German-speaking countries, the participants chose English songs to sing. I found this curious, but I didn't question my groups about this. One year I was teaching in Switzerland during the summer solstice. I wanted to perform a short ceremony with the group to honor the change of season. I asked participants of the group to create a short song they could sing to honor the earth. Once again people sang English songs that they had learned from a tape or through other workshops. Finally I stopped the ceremony and asked that people please create a new song that they had not heard and to sing it in their own language. Not much came from anyone in the group after that request. A few days later we were doing a healing ceremony. We were celebrating the success of the healings that had taken place by singing songs we loved. Again there were only English songs sung. What troubled me was not that they weren't singing in German; indeed, the experience can be more freeing and powerful when one sings in another language. What concerned me was the lack of spontaneity and passion. I finally called out, "Where are all the German songs?" A woman responded, "They were taken from us during the Inquisition."

Whether this is true or not, it gave me something to think about. Many of us lost power in our lives and our own connection with divine forces when we were told not to sing because we had a terrible voice, or that we were not creative and couldn't write a song, or that only certain songs were appropriate and beautiful to sing.

Today many people complain of feeling a lack of power in their bodies and in their lives. I have found through my own spiritual practice that by singing any one of my power songs, I not only feel expansive, but also get a concrete feeling of tremendous power, felt as life force and energy filling my body. I advise my clients and students who complain about depression and powerlessness to sing a power song of their creation. It works every time.

○ EXERCISES

The next step in experiencing union with your creator is to compose a short song that you can sing when you want this to occur. Take some of the key words from your story and put them together to form a song. Or begin with words and allow a hum to evolve from those words that will put you in an expanded state of consciousness.

I find working in nature helpful in finding a song, since it puts you in touch with spirit. Take a walk in nature or sit by a tree where you know you won't be disturbed. Think about the key words and concepts of your creation story and begin to sing. As you sing your story, a concise, melodious song will evolve. Keep singing this song or humming the melody until you really experience your ego dissolving and you have the experience of losing yourself in union with all of life and your creator. I have found toning (chanting sustained vowel sounds) evolving from my song especially powerful in placing me in the "hollow bone" state, allowing me to embody the energy for transmutation to occur.

Continue working with this song until you really experience divine love and essence. Then experiment with using song in your practice and your life, but please use it only when appropriate, such as for your own spiritual meditation and the healing of yourself and others. Do not try to have a union experience while driving. This is one place where the ego is necessary. Don't use your song when you have a need to truly experience space and time. Singing, really singing, in a strong voice will always bring you to a place of spirit, allowing you to experience union with source.

Another effective tool to connect with the power of the universe is dance. Although most of us are familiar with the power of dance, many of us have issues around not being a dancer or being clumsy. Such inhibitions, however, come from the unfortunate tendency in our culture to compare ourselves to others instead of truly honoring and enjoying our own experiences. Being able to move your body will definitely put you in physical connection with the creator, since dance, like song, creates the experience of expansion and embracing all of life. When you can truly allow your body to move without self-consciousness, complete union with the divine and with life will be the result. When you can dance with complete abandon, the experience of ecstasy occurs. Ecstasy is union with the divine.

In *A Fall to Grace,* a fiction work describing my own spiritual journey, the main character, C Alexandra, speaks to her teacher, the Egyptian goddess Isis, about the power of dance to connect the self to the spirit world.

Isis says: For people to experience true happiness, they must learn to reconnect with the source and with nature. . . . You like to dance, don't you?

Entranced by the streetlights and pitter-patter of the rain, I answer indifferently, Yes, I do. But I haven't danced in quite a while.

Think back to when you had a good time dancing with a partner.

I can remember one of those times.

To create beautiful dance movements with a partner, one must be fully engaged in the dance. Can you imagine what would happen if you were constantly looking around at what others were doing?

I wouldn't be able to connect with my partner.

Exactly. Your dance with the spirits you have met is beautiful, and it will continue. Your earth dance with your own soul and with nature can also be beautiful. What you must learn is to stay engaged with your partners, the rhythms, and the movements. Don't worry about what others are doing. Instead, show them how to find their own dancing partners in the spirit world and the world of nature.[8]

Although Isis is using dance as a metaphor for life, let us take what she says here literally for a moment. Taken this way, the passage can help us see the necessity of bringing our creation story into our body and allowing ourselves to fully participate in the experience of dance without judging our ability or appearance.

○ EXERCISES

Sing your song or hum the melody of your creation story. As you sing or hum, allow movements that reflect your creation myth to emerge. While you dance your story of life and creation, meditate on the symbol that you created as an emblem of the story. End your dance by allowing yourself to merge with the symbol. Hold this position for as long as you can, merging the visual symbol with your body.

Remember the original intention set forth in the Introduction, which is to open the doors between nonordinary reality and ordinary reality so that spirit, the compassionate spirits, and the gods and goddesses can once again join us on earth for the purpose of transmutation. Song and dance create the energy that allows the spirits to come through the doorway.

If you do all the exercises that go with this part of the book you have done a lot. Take some time for all this to settle. Continue your meditation on the symbol, experimenting with how the use of song and dance can facilitate the experience of union with the divine, the source of life. How does this feel to you? How does this change your life? How does this change your perceptions about yourself and others? How do you use this to heal yourself? How do you use this to heal others? Have any miracles occurred since you began this process? Keep notes on your experiences. As you attain a higher consciousness it will be fascinating for you to look back on the beginning of your adventure with transmutation.

Another way to attain perspective on this process is to share your practices with friends. Group sharing of personal creation myths is enlightening and encourages respect for a range of other individuals. The Mojave shamans of Arizona do this. Once a year they gather and stay up all night, sharing and singing their various creation myths. When morning comes, they all remark on how beautiful it was to hear each story.

Unfortunately, in our culture often we get stuck in the belief that there is only one truth and thus only one way of perceiving such things as creation. However, life is infinitely richer when we can acknowledge that we all have different perspectives, which in totality create an elaborate tapestry of the beauty of life.

AS WITHIN, SO WITHOUT

All esoteric traditions embrace the belief "As above, so below; as within, so without"—the understanding that if God created humankind in his own image, then God lives inside us as well as outside us. In today's culture the search for God inside ourselves seems to be accelerating. Years ago I had a dream in which a voice delivered this message: "Man has been looking for God outside of himself for the last two thousand years. Man will be looking for God inside of himself for the next two thousand years."

My life has been very full with spiritual experiences. Most have come from my own shamanic journey practice. Early on in my shamanic work I decided to journey to "the light." The question I had for "the light" was: "Why can I only experience you while I am on drugs or near death?" I could experience the absolute divine love of the light only while I was in an extreme situation. To my surprise, "the light" responded to me. Up to then my only experience of "the light" had been impersonal. "The light" responded: "As long as you have an ego, you cannot experience me outside of yourself. To experience me, you must go as deep inside of yourself as you travel outside to find me."

On drugs and during my NDEs I experienced ego death. The profound advice of "the light" was that now I had to journey inside myself to truly find God. For me, this means going to the deep, still, and silent place inside myself. I use singing, journeying, meditating, and movement practices such as yoga and chi gong to accomplish this task.

Sometimes we must reach inside ourselves to let our own divinity shine through.

O E X E R C I S E S

To learn to use inner contact with the divine in your own healing, first lie quietly in bed or on the floor. You might want to put on some music that will stop mental chatter and help you expand your consciousness. Close your eyes and meditate on an image or symbol of the divine that you have been working with. Breathe slowly but naturally. Allow your breathing to take you deeper into your experience. Try to experience the power of the universe, the absolute inside yourself. When you can truly experience the divine, God, the goddess, inside you, place your hand somewhere on your body where you feel pain. This might be a physical pain, an emotional pain living in your heart, or even fear in your solar plexus. With your breath, let the experience of your own divinity come through to your hands to heal your pain.

Stay with the experience until you get a sense that this is enough for now. Then slowly, with your breath, begin to come back to an ordinary state of consciousness. Allow yourself to relax and be still while opening your eyes. Take some time to reflect on your experience.

To heal the earth through transmutation, you must be able to merge with the divine in you as well as around you.

Parts of the formula for transmutation used here:

Intention: You must intend to merge with the divine to have an experience of union.

Love: Being in union with the absolute creates the true experience of divine love. Love heals.

Harmony: To be in union with the creator, you must move in harmony with yourself and the rest of life.

Focus: You must keep a strong focus on your intention to experience union.

Union: Union with the divine who created us and with your own divinity is the main key to transmutation.

Concentration: The more you can concentrate and meditate on your symbol for the power of the universe, the more it will manifest in your life.

Imagination: You must be able to imagine not only your own creation myth and your symbol of the divine, but also that you have the ability to manifest this healing power in your life, the lives of others, and the planet.

II

Separation versus Union

Imagine you are feeling disconnected from yourself, the rest of life, and your creator. You have lost your center and some of yourself to other people's projections and negativity.

How can you get back to the truth of what you know? You are one with your creator as well as part of a greater whole. You take a few deep breaths, settling back into yourself. As you settle you bring forth the symbol of your creator, breathe it into yourself, and breathe it back to the universe.

Your unconscious reveals to you what you think is most precious: a sound, a sight, a feeling, a taste, a smell—something that touches your soul and helps you remember the joy of living on earth. You remember your beauty. You sing a song that helps you harmonize with yourself and the rest of life. This song helps still your thoughts and brings you to a place of power and silence.

    You feel home again, connected again. You've transmuted your troubles of the day to a state of peace and harmony. You remember your ever-present connection with the source of all life.

3

Remembering Our Connection

When an inner situation is not made conscious,
it appears as fate.

— CARL JUNG

It would be wonderful if we could always stay in a state of ecstasy connected with the divine. However, although the spiritual part of ourselves could maintain such a state, the egoic part could not. The nature of the ego is to feel separate. We become locked into ourselves and experience isolation. Such feelings of isolation can lead to loneliness, insecurity, fear, or anger. Underneath all anger lies fear. These are all symptoms of feeling separate from the divine and the divinity that lives inside of each of us. It is our egoism that prevents us from remembering the truth of who we are.

To access the path to transmutation, we need to be in touch with both our shadow side and our spiritual side. We need to acknowledge our shadow side—feelings of fear, anger, envy, judgment, insecurity, loneliness, and so on. To devote all our energy to this side makes us self-absorbed in our egoic states. If we choose to spend our life exploring only our shadow side, we will not gain knowledge of our soul, which is crucial in learning to perform miracles in our lives. However, the reverse is also true: If we focus only on our spiritual side and do not acknowledge the dark places that live in us, the path to transmutation will also be closed.

As the East Indian sage Krishnamurti said, all the "drawers" must be opened and inspected to understand the illusion of the ego. Egoic states are illusory, because the truth is that we are not separate from the divine. Any voices inside us that state a different opinion have come from old authority voices of the past and illusory beliefs about ourselves.

Exploring our shadow side heightens our awareness about what keeps us from loving ourselves and others. There can be no union without love, and there can be no transmutation without union. Therefore, we must be diligent in searching for anything that inhibits love, such as fear.

The Egyptian goddess Sekhmet teaches humankind about the shadow. Whenever I meet Sekhmet in my meditations, she says: "All life is of the light." We must be able to acknowledge the dark places inside ourselves, without judgment, and bring light into the darkness, a process that is true transmutation. I believe that it is our humanness that keeps us compassionate. While there are spiritual traditions that teach transcendence of all egoic states, I feel it is important to honor our human nature while simultaneously remembering who we really are and the illusory nature of the ego.

The egoic states of suffering give us compassion for the rest of life. It is interesting to note that shamans are called "wounded healers," meaning they have a wound that never heals, which keeps the shaman's heart open to understanding the suffering of others.

So we need to be compassionate while at the same time knowing that our suffering does not reflect the truth of who we are. For transmutation to occur, we must know our soul and our connection to the divine. On the other hand, since love is a key to transmutation, we must not exist in a state of spiritual arrogance, but always maintain compassion.

Life is a constant spiritual practice. It is not like an exercise program in which you see results after working out three times a week. To have the power for transmutation, you must try to be infused with spirit twenty-four hours a day, seven days a week, 365 days a year. Yes, you can still have fun—that's all part of the adventure.

It is not sufficient to focus on your spiritual life for only an hour a day and then the rest of the day be a stressed-out, raging person or one consumed with fear. The ability to transmute requires a full-time commitment to connection with spirit, giving it the space to dance through your life whenever appropriate, not just at times you designate. In this way you integrate the spiritual side of life into your ordinary life, which creates an opening for the spirits to once again roam the earth, dissolving the veils between the worlds.

While living a functional life in society, it is really not possible for us to stay in a constant state of union with spirit. We do need to return to an egoic state while in the back of our mind remembering our spiritual connection.

When you embark on a spiritual practice of unity with the divine and the rest of life, you will find that, as in nature, there is an ebb and flow to your practice. There will be times when it is easy to feel a strong connection with the spirit that lives in all things. During other periods you may experience frustration or anger when you have difficulty making such a connection. When you are in a complete experience of union, the ego dies. The nature of union is that there is no separation. However, the ego sometimes rebels and may begin acting out, sabotaging your thoughts and actions. You no longer feel compassionate toward your fellow humans. You might find yourself being short or grumpy with people.

Such reactions are natural. We are part of nature rather than separate from nature. Life consists of an ebb and flow. We can't be perfectly attuned to divinity all the time. However, I will share some things you can work with during these times to quiet the threatened ego. I will also share things you can do during these times to remind yourself who you truly are beyond your ego and to bring meaning back into your life. Remember, the intention of our work is to create an energetic opening, allowing spirit and the spirits to dance with us.

We have choices in our interactions with other people and in the attitude with which we embrace our life. However, we often go on automatic and don't stop to make conscious choices. Frequently we choose to react instead of remaining conscious. Therefore it is essential that we become more aware during our interactions. One of the keys to making appropriate choices is staying conscious in the present.

This does not mean that people won't project their feelings of fear and anger onto us. But we can't be responsible for people misinterpreting our words and actions; we can take responsibility only for our behavior.

In many spiritual traditions, pursuing a spiritual path is described as walking on a razor's edge. There are many ways to fall off the edge, such as judging yourself or others, not acting out of harmony, compromising your integrity, acting out of spiritual arrogance, not respecting yourself and the rest of life, etc. I am sure you get the point.

Constant diligence and attention are required to walk the edge. If you do fall off, it is important to get back on the path by changing your self-talk and thoughts.

In a shamanic journey I received this powerful message: "Don't forget in the dark what you learned in the light." The following material will help you with this.

TOOLS FOR REMEMBERING OUR CONNECTION

When we find ourselves reacting instead of making conscious choices, we have usually lost our center. One of the most powerful ways to return to a centered place or to stay centered throughout the day is by watching our breathing. When you move into reactivity or lose your center or focus, your breathing becomes shallow.

Breathing slowly and deeply throughout the day is one way to keep your spiritual connection with the divine strong. According to Ron Roth, mystical religions have invested a great deal of time to understand the concept of breath in the spiritual dimension, as mystics see spirit as the breath of God. In Genesis, it is the creative breath of God that generates life. The breath later on would be described as Holy Spirit. St. Paul said it was the breath of God that raised Jesus from the dead. This same breath is in each of us and can make our bodies well and congruent with our spirit and soul.[1]

Robert Gass shows us that by looking at the root words for *breath* and *soul,* we can see how both words are interconnected. The Greek word for "soul" is *psyche,* which comes from the root *psychein,* meaning "to breathe." In Hebrew the word for "breath," *ruach,* means "spirit." In Latin the word for "soul" is *anima,* and "spirit" is *animus,* which both derive from *anemos,* the word for "wind." The Zen master Thich Nhat Hanh says that the breath is "the bridge that connects life to consciousness."[2]

To gain greater awareness of your connection with the divine, as you go about your day try to notice how your breathing is altered as your mental and emotional states change—for example, if something or someone upsets you, if you experience fear, or if you feel uncentered.

The following chapters include some other tools to assist you in remaining conscious during your interactions with others while also helping shift your attitude about life. This next part is divided into three chapters to aid your work with the material.

As you work with what is written, let your intuition guide you in knowing the truth that comes up for you with all the exercises. Truth is something you know in your bones. If you need an exercise to help you get in touch with this, I have placed one in the Appendix for you.

Unfortunately, in our culture, we don't often allow ourselves the space or time to go inside ourselves long enough to distinguish truth from mental chatter. Instead we often get lost in our insecurities and fears, or we lose ourselves in other people's projections. Consequently we must learn how to become centered and sit inside ourselves. External changes will manifest in our lives through internal change. Inner harmony creates outer harmony.

When we open up to our own intuitive knowing, we find that profound changes begin to happen in our lives when we least expect them. If we don't try so hard to make things change, we are often caught by surprise when changes happen on their own. Albert Einstein said that when you follow your intuition, "the solutions come to you, and you don't know how or why."

4

Remembering the Beauty

A common revelation reported by dying people is how precious life is. By contrast, a common regret of people near death is that they wish they had appreciated life more fully. However, we don't have to be literally near death to have this experience. We can learn how to appreciate our lives daily.

In addition to needing a personal creation story, we must also need a deep appreciation for life for transmutation to happen.

○ EXERCISES

In your mind conjure up images, sensations, sounds, smells, and tastes that invoke the feeling of the preciousness of life. Some examples might be:

* A beautiful flower whose color, smell, and beauty fill you with awe for life
* The smile of a baby
* The playfulness of a kitten, puppy, or other young animal that makes you feel joyful
* A waterfall
* The magic of a dragonfly or of bees pollinating

- An ant carrying ten times its own weight in food
- A miraculous tree growing out of rock
- The smell of your favorite food cooking
- The sound or smell of rain
- The taste of something sweet or savory

Think of other personal things that make you recall how precious life is. Concentrate on some of these thoughts when you lose your center. For example, become aware of them when you feel your temper flaring, when you find yourself driven by rage, or when you question the meaning of life.

If you take just one second to bring an image, feeling, sound, smell, or taste into your consciousness, this will immediately change your mood. You might not be in a complete state of ecstasy, but you will be in greater harmony with life.

REMEMBERING THE TRUE NATURE OF OUR SOUL

In workshops I am often asked to define the difference between soul and spirit. It is impossible to state a definitive distinction and proclaim one truth about such a complex issue. Philosophical schools have been addressing that for eons. I can only relate what is true for me. In my view, spirit is the part of myself that can never be hurt. It is the exact image of the divine; it is perfect, doesn't need to evolve, and doesn't need to be healed. My spirit lives inside me in a state of complete perfection and will endure after my body has ceased to exist. It knows how to create, as God does; it knows how to heal. It is just divine essence. My task is to learn through my continued spiritual practice how to find that place deep inside myself and access its inherent knowing. This is the part of me that must be revealed for transmutation of illness and toxins to occur.

By contrast, my soul is the essence of myself that came into the world to grow and evolve. My soul came into this world to have adventures. My soul will survive after my body's death to encounter new lessons and opportunities when it is reborn once again into the world.

Although there are various spiritual philosophies that would not agree with my definitions, the important thing is that I have found a way to comprehend what part of me was made in the image of the creator and what part of me evolves over time.

After I had been teaching and working with soul retrieval for some years, another aspect of the work began to emerge. In soul retrieval I find the portion of a person's essence that has left the body as a result of trauma. In most shamanic cultures around the world, it is believed that when we suffer an emotional or physical trauma a piece of our soul, or essence, leaves our body in order to survive the experience. The psychological term for this is *dissociation*. In psychology we don't speak about what dissociates or where that part goes, but simply about the process.

For thousands of years shamans have understood that this piece of our soul flees to the invisible worlds of nonordinary reality. In my first book, *Soul Retrieval: Mending the Fragmented Self,* I describe this process in depth. Briefly, soul loss is a survival mechanism. It is how our psyche survives pain. For example, if I was going to be in a head-on car collision, the very last place that I would want to be at the point of impact was in my body, because my psyche could not withstand that kind of pain.

Events that would cause soul loss are physical, emotional, and sexual abuse; surgery; being in an accident; wartime stress; experiencing a disaster, such as a hurricane, fire, or earthquake; addictions; death of a loved one; or divorce. Actually, anything that causes shock can cause soul loss.

It was through my work with soul retrieval that I became aware of the importance of gaining knowledge of a soul's purpose in the world. I was teaching soul retrieval around the world, and had seen over a thousand clients, when my work took a new direction. What began occurring was that while I was in a journey and being shown what a client lost, I was also shown why the soul entered the world in the first place—the true essence of my client's soul and the life purpose that my client had forgotten. Further, I was shown the gifts, talents, and strengths my client brought into the world to manifest in this lifetime. This I called soul remembering instead of soul retrieval.

All this was revealed to me by my own helping spirits as a symbol, which I could bring back with the lost soul parts I had found. I could draw or paint this symbol for my client so that he or she could meditate on it throughout the day in the same manner that I described working with the power and potential of symbols earlier.

When I wrote *Welcome Home* and included a section on soul remembering, I had no idea how important this work would become for me. In the beginning, I only occasionally performed a soul remembering, but as my work with soul retrieval continued, soul remembering began to predominate in my practice.

Another shift in the focus of my shamanic work occurred as a result of the need for modern adaptation. I think that one of the reasons the practice of shamanism has survived for at least forty thousand years is that the compassionate spirits evolve the healing work in accordance with people's changing needs.

I found that there were consequences of performing soul retrieval in a psychologically sophisticated culture such as ours. People became psychologically stuck in the details of their soul loss instead of embracing the healing offered by the return of lost essence. This is the real purpose of a soul retrieval, rather than getting mired in the story.

However, my helping spirits remedied this problem by showing me less about the cause of the soul loss and more about the gifts that were being returned to the client. They also began to show me the original, true essence of the client, which had been forgotten.

I network with the people who study with me, as we are all pioneers in reintroducing this ancient technique. Amazingly, I found that at exactly the same time my work evolved, so did the work of fellow practitioners. What this taught me was how the spirits will alter the work to fit the needs of people.

What do we need right now in our culture? Do we need to go over and over what happened to us? Yes, of course, if we have never looked at our past. But for those of us who have been going over and over the same story, is it time to move on?

We all need inspiration. We need to have the fire inside reignited and to have our excitement for life renewed. A great way to receive such inspiration is to learn why our soul originally decided to be born into this world. We can approach this by asking ourselves such questions as the following: What is the nature of our soul? What are the gifts, talents, and strengths we came into this world to manifest in this lifetime? Who were we before we were told who we are?

The need for understanding our soul's original purpose is important, because in our culture our true mission is often obscured. We often define ourselves by what other people project onto us. We are told by families, teachers, and authority figures who we are supposed to be and what we are good at. We are then loved for what we do rather than for who we are. Thus our original essence becomes buried deep within ourselves, and we lose contact with who we really are— a situation that causes depression and lack of excitement for life along with a variety of other consequences.

One example of the consequences of this is the following story: A man traveled to see me for some shamanic healing work. When he entered my office, I was struck by his incredible power of presence. We didn't speak much, since he just wanted me to journey for him without giving me any information, a method I actually prefer. Since in shamanic healing work the helping spirits, not me, decide what is needed, it is best simply to take the name of the client to the spirits and remain open about what happens.

In this case, I journeyed to the home of my power animal. He explained to me that this man needed a soul remembering. Further, he said that when this man came into the world, his purpose was to bring forth the energy of the divine feminine and heal by just being. I thought of the Buddhist story of the person who changes the world by sitting under a tree. We don't always have to be active externally to change the world; we can do so through introspection and meditation.

I told my power animal that because my client was so obviously male, I couldn't go back to this man blowing into his body the divine feminine principle of healing and changing the world by just being. However, my power animal demanded that I follow instructions. Consequently I returned blowing into this man a symbol I was shown of pure feminine energy, and I gave him the information provided by my power animal.

Stunned by what I had been shown, my client related his story. As a child, his power of presence had been recognized by his family and teachers, and as a result, he had been pushed into being very active in the world and manifesting his male dynamic energy. His leadership abilities were honed, and later he was urged to attend law school and then pursue politics. However, what his own soul yearned for was to change and heal the world by sitting with a tree. My power animal had validated his true nature, which authority figures around him had covered up with their own projection of how they saw him.

In *A Fall to Grace* I use the metaphor of sculpture to describe how forgetting true essence feels. I describe how the projections, beliefs, attitudes, judgment, and feelings put upon me by family, authority figures, friends, and strangers are like clay being flung onto a sculpture. Before too long the figurine, forged by others, no longer contains the truth of who I am. As the clay hardens I feel an unnatural tension and become weighed down by the rules of society, the projections cast by others, and the negative feelings in the world around me. The stresses I put myself through create an opening for emotional and physical illness to enter.[1]

We will look in the next section at how becoming passionate

about our life keeps illness out of our body. But for now we must remember who we truly are. The sad truth is that no one in an ordinary state of consciousness sees us for who we really are. The nature of the ego and mind is to project an image onto others that is not accurate, but rather reflects our own needs, emotional states, or beliefs. We project onto others what we want to see rather than what is true. The absolute, the compassionate spirits, and you are the only beings who can see you for all you are. The absolute and the compassionate spirits already know your true nature. The work for you is to discover the nature of your true essence.

According to John Anthony West, who writes and lectures on ancient Egypt, the goal of life for the ancient Egyptians was to transform the soul. Most important was to evolve from the "material beings that we are by birth to the spiritual beings that we are by birthright." The Egyptians' doctrine, their temples, their tombs, and all they did were directed toward this goal.[2]

People are so out of touch with their beauty and essence that the veils of reality are clouded over. You must honor yourself and your own beauty before you can truly see it in the earth. Once you can do that, the veils of illusion begin to lift, and once again you can see the perfection in all things.

○ EXERCISES

Try to discover what adventure you signed up for in choosing to be born. What are the gifts, talents, and strengths you came into this world to manifest? What is the nature of your true essence? Who are you beyond who you were told by others that you are? Who are you beyond what society projects onto you?

If you already have your own spiritual practice where you can divine information for yourself, meditate or journey on these questions. If you don't have a way of receiving information, here are some suggestions about how to access this information:

* Before you go to bed, ask for a dream that will reveal this information. Dreaming is a wonderful way of tapping into your own intuitive knowledge. When asking for a dream, you may need to be persistent—one might not come the first night you ask.

* Take a walk in nature. Choose a place where you are already familiar with the landscape so that you do not spend your time sightseeing and can instead move into a meditative state of consciousness. Before you begin your walk, have the intention of wanting to be shown your true essence. Notice what comes to you through your own intuitive knowledge. Notice if you receive an image, if you have a feeling that reveals this information to you, or if you actually get a direct revelation through words that come to you.

* You can also meditate at home to discover this information. Lie down or sit in a comfortable position. Put on some music which will put you in an expanded state of consciousness. One of the pieces of music I use is Pachelbel's Canon in D. Years ago it was discovered that this music aided superlearning by inducing a deep meditative state of consciousness. Many different kinds of music will do this. Find music that works for you. As you listen to the music you have selected, allow your body to relax. Hold the question you would like an answer to in your mind. Don't think about it, just keep holding it. Allow yourself to move into a deep meditative state. Allow an answer to come to you. The answer might take many forms: You might see an image, hear words, feel sensations in your body, or experience a combination of these. If you allow yourself to really relax while holding the question, some answer will come. If you find yourself hearing the voice of an authority figure from your past, you are not in a deep enough state of meditation. Try to get past all mental chatter and negative voices by just acknowledging their presence and moving on.

Fighting such voices only adds fuel to the fire and makes them stronger.

* You can also try to do some automatic writing or drawing. Sit down and write your question on a piece of paper. Then watch what comes. Again, putting on some consciousness-expanding music will help with this process.

If you did not get a symbol along with the information you received, try to find one. You can use the same ways to access information described above, or you can just imagine a symbol that will represent the knowledge you received.

Draw or paint a picture of this symbol, and put it in a place where you will see it all the time. Let the symbol speak to your psyche and permeate your being.

Over the years of working with this process in my own life, a variety of meaningful symbols have emerged. I already described the symbolic painting of light I use to remind myself of the divine forces in and around me. The five-pointed star is another symbol that helps me remember the truth of who I am. I drink water out of a glass decorated with stars, and have the symbol up in a variety of places in my house. The picture of a rose came forth next to describe an aspect of my being. I not only keep roses around me, but also purchase rose oil so that I can take in the smell of my true being.

Being surrounded by these different pictures and objects gives me constant reminders of my true essence, especially as I lose myself to expectations and projections from the outside world. I surround myself with portraits that reflect back to me the truth of who I am.

When you feel disconnected from your source and from others, focus on your personal symbol and remember who you truly are. This process will reconnect you with yourself and with the world around you again, as well as reempower you when you feel disempowered by people or events in your daily life.

Life without meaning results in despair. A life devoid of passion causes disease, whereas passion creates vitality. A life without passion is not vital. In *Welcome Home* I discussed spiritual healing work done with a woman who had AIDS. Here I again briefly recount that case study, as the message I received from working with this woman was the most profound teaching I have received about the nature of illness.

AIDS was the third life-threatening illness my client had experienced. As a child, she had Hodgkin's disease; as a young adult, she had a rare brain parasite; and as a woman in her thirties, she had contracted the virus that causes AIDS.

I performed a soul retrieval for her. The shamanic journey was very powerful and vivid. The spirits set up a cartoon scene to drive the point home. I saw the picture of a suburban neighborhood where everything was completely filled with the joy of life. The bright yellow sun in the sky was beaming down on the earth. The houses all had smiling faces and were swaying back and forth in the joy of their earth dance. The birds were singing. The cars parked on the streets were laughing and dancing. The colors were surrealistically bright.

My client, age three, arrived on the scene riding a tricycle. She was cycling down the street with no affect on her face. She just looked dispassionately from side to side as she rode.

Finally my power animal shared this auditory message with me: "The cause of her illness was apathy, and the cure was passion. Her lesson in this lifetime was what happened when another life form in her body had more passion for life than she did. It took over."

Although my client ultimately did pass away, she left me with an incredible message to share with the world. For I don't see that we live lives filled with passion, meaning, and creativity. After all, in school we were taught not to stand out or cause trouble, and that there are only a few creative geniuses in the world—excluding us. Sound familiar?

Is it that we have deadened ourselves as we became socialized? Does this deadening make us vulnerable to passionate bacteria and viruses that want to live more than we do?

Part of our adventure in the transmutation process is bringing meaning and passion back into our lives. There is no way to perform the miracle of transforming illness and toxins without a strong will not only to survive, but to live with passion.

One night while teaching a workshop in the Santa Cruz mountains, I took a long walk back from dinner to the meeting room and looked up at the night sky. It had been raining for days, and this was the first night I could see the stars. Since I was from New Mexico, where the mind is boggled by all the stars in the night sky, I found myself searching for them. Finally I saw a lone star in the sky. At that moment I had a realization. When a group of people are gathered outside at night, no one seems to get excited when there are only a few stars shining, but when the sky is lit up with billions of stars, the excitement is electrifying. In observing this, I wondered why it was that we believe that on earth there can be only a few shining stars, a few individuals who excel. Aren't we all a reflection of the light we see in the night sky? Has anyone ever said: "I wish so many stars weren't shining so brightly"? Isn't our excitement about how *many* stars are shining simultaneously? When you were a child, did anyone ever tell you not to shine so brightly, not to bring so much attention to yourself?

When we don't know our own shine, our earth dance becomes filled with insecurity. This can be expressed through competitiveness, feelings of alienation, and loneliness.

Wouldn't it be wonderful if we all made a decision to act contrary to our socialization process and ignite the light inside of ourselves to shine as brightly as we can? Can you imagine the beauty that would shine here on earth and be reflected back to the heavens? It is okay to shine as brightly as we can. It is our birthright to fully express our souls, although it takes some soul searching to discover how we can truly manifest the essence we brought into this world. We can begin by meditating on this question: "What would bring passion and meaning back into my life again?"

In the New Testament, particularly in the Sermon on the Mount, Jesus charges his listeners to be the salt of the earth and not to hide their lights under baskets (Matthew 5:13–20). Presbyterian minister Jennifer Rike spoke about shining light in our lives in one of her sermons. She says that with the three images of salt, city, and light, Jesus challenges us to be good and faithful servants of God and Christ by shining our light in the world. We must shine even if it means bringing misunderstanding and persecution. We must manifest the grace we have received, no matter what the cost. This involves shining our light in ways that flow naturally and not making ourselves into something we are not. We don't need to seek out places to shine; we just need to express the light and love that are always in us.[3]

Another side of finding passion and meaning is what Jack Schwarz calls acquiring and maintaining radiance. He says if you maintain a high enough energy field around you, disease will not affect you.[4]

He advises us to get joy and love out of life every day and to accept change as an exciting challenge. When we move away from living in a state of fear and anxiety, stop defending ourselves against enemies and disease, and encircle ourselves with our expanding, radiant energy, we can resonate with each other in a healthy state of spiritual power.[5]

Schwarz reminds us that we must see that the power to heal is in ourselves, in our beingness, spirit, and energy. He shares his experience of being on the battlefield in World War II. Many people were shot and never noticed the pain. In 1940 a hospital in Rotterdam was bombed, causing great destruction. As the ceiling gave way and windows shattered, some patients who had been bedridden for ten to fifteen years suddenly jumped up, pulled out life support tubes, and ran in bare feet over broken glass and through flames to safety. Even their clothes remained untouched. These patients exhibited the capability for self-healing, a capability that all of us have today.[6]

When we maintain our energy, radiance, and health, we can help those who come into our presence. Some people lack the knowledge and experience to regenerate themselves. Schwarz uses the metaphor of feeling as if one is stalled in the Sahara. Those of us who have maintained our energy can be seen as "cosmic AAA" and can act as jumper cables. You cannot give your energy to anyone, but with your high energy you can activate their low energy. In this way they can regenerate themselves—this the true art of healing.[7]

We all need inspiration right now. We all need to find our own light and know it is okay to shine it in the world. And we must plant seeds of love and hope as we find meaning and passion and shine our essence in the world. Not only will we heal ourselves, but we will be an inspiration for others in need.

An important aspect of having passion for life is knowing that there is a future and looking forward to it. In *Man's Search for Meaning* Victor Frankl, a psychiatrist who survived the concentration camps of the Holocaust, described the horrors of his experience and the key to his survival. After his release he developed an approach to psychotherapy known as logotherapy.

Frankl believes that the motivational life force is humankind's search for meaning. He says that those who knew a task was waiting for them were most apt to survive in the Nazi concentration camps. He quotes the wise words of Nietzsche: "He who has a why to live can bear almost any *how*." Frankl came to the same conclusion that has been reached by other authors of books on concentration camps, and by psychiatric investigators into Japanese, North Korean, and North Vietnamese prisoner-of-war camps.[8]

One of Victor Frankl's most important observations is that having a future to look forward to is necessary for survival. This has also been my experience. Over the years I have met five people who were originally HIV positive but who have since tested HIV negative. I quizzed all these people, trying to identify any common thread to their healing. What I discovered was that they shared both the devout belief that they would have a positive future and the ability to imagine such a future.

I have also seen my own parents defy debilitation through a similar positive outlook. They are now eighty-five, and life is no longer easy for them, but they have an incredible will to survive. Whenever I speak to my mother, the conversation is dominated by what my parents are looking forward to—simple things, not life goals. For example, they might talk about a friend or a movie they are going to see, or a short trip they plan to take—just something to look forward to besides sitting in the living room staring at the walls. I have realized that this is an important tool in their effort to avoid being overwhelmed by the problems of old age.

I am not trying to oversimplify the healing process, but visioning a positive future seems to be a key factor in transmutation and healing. To transform problems in our lives, we need to know that there is a good future to look forward to.

However, this does not mean that we should live in the future. All spiritual traditions teach the importance of living in the present, and we should remember that our future is created from the present. A teacher of mine advised me once to "only look as far as the headlights are shining." A driver who tries to see beyond where the light is shining is in danger of driving off the road.

I have a spiritual teacher who keeps reminding me that life is an adventure and that I need to stop taking everything so seriously. When she first told me this, I responded by asking her to comment on some catastrophes that could happen to me. Afterward I revealed my worst fear: "What if I end up a bag lady on the streets of New York?" She looked off into the distance for a moment, then gazed intensely at me and with a twinkle in her eyes responded: "What an amazing adventure that would be."

At first this reply shocked me, but after carefully considering her response, I understood the point: What an incredible life experience that would be.

Life is to be experienced in its fullest. Every experience we have can be filled with great teachings and opportunities. If we make a commitment to experience life to its fullest and live with passion and meaning, the light that we shine will naturally create an energy of transmutation. Thus pain, anger, and fear can be transmuted into wonderment, excitement, and joy. In this regard we are all creative geniuses.

○ EXERCISES

When I ask what would bring passion and meaning into people's lives, at first they often respond with a blank stare or frown. Most people don't know where to start. Then once I get people to begin imagining options, a new challenge frequently appears: They come up with such ambitious, overwhelming goals that there is no way to reach them. Consequently they sometimes get paralyzed by the vision instead of inspired and empowered.

In looking at what would bring passion and meaning into your life, start with a goal that is attainable. Once you see that you can succeed walking down this path, you can then set larger goals. There are no rules, since you have your whole life to live. Living a life filled with passion and meaning is not an exercise but a process. Be patient with yourself as you discover your route.

Take some time to either walk in nature or create a quiet space alone in your house. Meditate or dream on these questions: What would bring passion and meaning back into your life? What can you begin to do tomorrow that would make you feel alive and excited?

Select a modest goal at first, such as taking more walks, enrolling in a class that sparks your interest (try tai chi, yoga, or painting), or reading some inspirational books. Use your imagination.

You might also brainstorm with friends or family about this, but don't give your power away to anyone else, and use them only for support, not as authority figures who tell you what to do. Reach inside to find out how to manifest your own creativity in the world.

Keep a journal of the insights you get, as well as any sabotaging self-doubt that comes up. Then you can perform some ceremony to release any beliefs or habits that are blocking you. (See Part VI for suggestions.)

We must learn to use our imagination to envision a future we can look forward to. We often envision a future of doom and gloom. As we watch the news and get caught up in the despair of our culture, it is important to realize that we have the power to change our lives and to inspire others to do the same.

To heal the earth through transmutation, you must appreciate your own life as well as the life of all living beings. You need to remember and embody your true nature. As you remember your perfection, the world around you will reflect that perfection back to you. Returning to a life filled with passion and meaning will give you the energy to heal your environment.

To heal the earth through transmutation, you must acknowledge that you have the power and knowledge to do so. Parts of the formula for transmutation used here:

Intention: You must hold the intention to remember who you truly are and to live a passionate life filled with

appreciation and meaning to transmute pain, toxins, and
the energy around you.

Love: You must love yourself and life enough to want to
change a destructive state of consciousness into a healing
state of consciousness.

Harmony: By conjuring up an image or sensation of the
preciousness of life, remembering the truth of who you
truly are beyond judgment and projection, and living a life
filled with passion and meaning, you will harmonize your
own energies as well as create harmony around you.

Union: To acknowledge the wondrousness of life and to
remember your true nature will naturally expand your
energy, shifting you into a state of union with the creator.

Focus: You must focus on the vision and attention needed to
manifest your intention.

Concentration: Life is a spiritual practice. You must
concentrate your efforts on living a life infused with spirit.
Concentration is needed to empower your intention to
change your state of consciousness.

Imagination: To transmute a negative state of frustration,
anger, or fear, you must be able to imagine an image,
smell, taste, sound, or sensation that will reaffirm the awe
of life. For transmutation to occur, you must be able to
imagine a truer self than you have previously been in
touch with. You must also be able to imagine yourself as a
creative genius who can transform your own life.

5

When Things Feel Bad

When you are listening to someone speak, you can hear words, but behind these words might be other thoughts and truer feelings. We often suspect that people are thinking and feeling something different from what they are actually saying, but we often do not think about or understand the energy that is created by this invisible communication. Further, we rarely consider the impact of all the negative thought forms we project onto others and into the airwaves as we go about our daily activities. Such invisible communication is not acknowledged in our culture but is well understood in all indigenous cultures, as is the difference between expressing anger and sending anger. If you have ever felt rage or experienced someone else's, you know that such negative energy is tangible. In fact, such energy can cause disease if you let it fill your body.

We constantly dump our anger, fear, frustrations, and despair. Sometimes we direct these emotions toward a person who we think is causing us pain, and other times we just release our negativity blindly into the air. In either case, such feelings have a definite impact on ourselves and others. Unfortunately, our earth and our immediate living and working environments have become invisible garbage dumps for all our pent-up feelings.

Ironically, the sickest people I work with in my own shamanic practice are psychotherapists. This is because we weren't taught in school how to shield ourselves from the negative energy projected by clients. Such emotions can cause negative thought forms that enter the bodies of people who don't know how to shield themselves.

We are all human, and unless we transcend the human condition, which is unlikely in our lifetime, we are subject to emotions. It is normal to be filled with emotion. As I have already said, the nature of the ego is to feel separate, and this experience of isolation causes feelings of fear, anger, despair, and frustration. Repressing these feelings results in energy blocks in our own body that cause illness, while blindly expressing our feelings creates a toxic environment for others.

We can, however, remedy this situation through the transmutation of negative energy. Transmuting negative energy is easy, and the results can be experienced immediately. This potent work is necessary for healing personal and environmental illness. Remember, in all interactions we have choices regarding how we respond to people and to life.

When you notice yourself having negative emotions, don't repress them, but allow yourself to honestly express your feelings. However, as you release the energy encompassing these feelings into the environment, ask that this energy be transformed into healing energy filled with light and love. It is just that simple.

When you have negative thoughts, you feed any illness that exists in your body; positive thoughts feed your body. You can use any of the methods already described to aid in transmuting the negative state you are in to a nurturing, life enhancing state.

When you are in a place where you feel that there is negative energy, allow yourself to feel your connection with your own true essence, the power of the divine, or the helping spirits you work with. Since there has to be a vacuum for negative energy to enter your body, if you are filled with power, there is no way that you can receive negative energy.

At first you will need to really concentrate on transmuting feelings and thought forms you are putting out and on shielding yourself from the negativity of others. However, once you have practiced this for a short while, the process will become more automatic. If you sometimes forget to transmute negativity, nothing terrible will happen. Practices take time and patience to perfect. Learning to behave in a new way always takes energy at first, before it becomes habitual.

Although we were raised in a culture where the energy of our communication is not acknowledged, it is time for us to realize that tangible energy is formed in all communication. The energy created through our words and thoughts goes somewhere; it doesn't just magically disappear. This energy can always be transmuted into a healing energy that embraces love. We need to incorporate this practice to enhance the quality of life for all beings.

One tool for transmuting the energy of our communications is confronting our emotions. In the practice of Taoism it is well understood that whenever there is an energy to be worked with, it is necessary to experience it fully for it to be transmuted—resisting the energy only strengthens it. For example, if I am angry and keep telling myself that it is unhealthy to be experiencing this emotion, my anger will only grow stronger. By contrast, if I experience my anger completely, it has no choice but to change. Once an emotional state is experienced completely, it is transformed.

Another tool for transmuting energy is control of breathing. As mentioned previously, you can use your breath to center yourself. When you are in an emotionally charged state, your breathing changes. If you slow your breathing down to a natural rhythm by taking deep breaths, you will be centered. Notice how you can accomplish this by taking three deep breaths.

Additionally, try transmuting negative emotions by thinking of a healing color. Experience this color moving all through the dark places inside yourself. You can also heal yourself by making an abstract drawing or painting using colors that are soothing to you. In these ways you can express your feelings but also transmute them.

There are many potent sitting and movement meditation practices, such as Vipassana meditation, Zen meditation, tai chi, chi gong, and yoga, that can help you with your breathing and learning how to center. These practices, of which I have named only a few, all promote the internal harmony and healing needed to create it in the external world. There are many resources and classes offered that you may wish to explore. It's important to find a practice that suits your personality and your physical ability as well as a teacher who honors your individual needs.

A further aspect of sending and transmuting negative energy is the manner in which we raise, pick or slaughter, and cook our food, since these actions may affect our attitude and health. Along with the actual food we are eating, we may be digesting the negativity from growers or harvesters, the fear of the animals that are killed, or the emotions of the cooks who prepare our food.

The book and movie *Like Water for Chocolate* depicted how we could ingest emotional substances with our food. It portrays a woman who is distressed about her sister marrying her true love. She is forced to cook and bake the food for her sister's wedding, and while she prepares each food and cake, she feels different emotions. Just as she cries over a dish while she is cooking it, the guests cry while they are eating it. As she laughs over a dish while cooking it, so do the guests while eating it.

In indigenous cultures food is harvested and animals slaughtered in an honoring manner. Dances and ceremonies are performed throughout the growing and harvesting process to beneficially influence food sources. And animals are killed in a way that would allow the least amount of adrenaline to enter their bloodstream.

Today most of us don't have full control over everything we eat. However, despite our lack of control over our food sources, we can pay attention to how we cook and eat our food. We can create a quiet, nurturing space for meals and not digest negativity by listening to the news or reading the paper while we eat. We can transmute the toxins in the food we eat through controlling our environment and by creating ceremonies in connection with our food. I will share these with you in Part VI, on ceremonies for transmutation.

Review the methods on using Taoist psychology, breathing, and color to transmute negative energy.

See your psyche as a lake or a piece of land. Visualize yourself swimming in the lake or hiking on the land. Notice how much garbage there is to pick up.

First practice transmuting feelings in a private, safe space before doing it in more public places. At the end of each day reflect on your events and interactions. If you get in touch with any negative emotions, allow them to arise. As you say, either out loud or silently, what you are feeling, add this phrase: "I ask that the energy from these emotions be transmuted to energy of healing, light, and love."

You might recall, for example, becoming irritated at an interaction with a coworker, feeling frustrated while you were in traffic, or being angry when an elevator door closed on you. You can replay the situation in your mind's eye. As you remember putting out a negative thought form, go back into the scene and silently say to yourself: "I ask that this energy be transformed to healing energy filled with love and light."

Further, you can remember a situation in which someone directed negativity toward you or in which you felt you picked some up. You can tune in to your own body and ask that any energy you absorbed be released to the universe and transmuted into healing energy filled with love and light.

It is also possible to protect yourself from negative energy in advance. Think about a symbol that imbues the qualities of protection and safety for you. Meditate on it to psychically surround yourself with a protective barrier when you feel you are being invaded by negative projections from others. Think about a symbol that imbues the qualities of protection and safety for you. Practice seeing yourself surrounded by this symbol. You might find that a color works better for you than a symbol. If so, surround yourself with this color.

To gain the benefit of positive energy, remain conscious of what energy you are projecting and what type is being directed at you. Then keep transmuting all energy that could possibly create illness for others or for yourself.

INQUIRY AND OBSERVATION

Two East Indian sages, Ramana Maharshi and Krishnamurti, taught very high-level spiritual practices important for work with transmutation. These practices are difficult to grasp at first and are, as Ramana Maharshi states, practices for the "ripe soul." Both approaches presented here will bring you to a similar place, but the methods are different. I cannot adequately describe the approaches of these two great sages in a short passage. But some of their basic method and philosophy is important to note in our work with transmutation.

Ramana Maharshi taught the practice of inquiry. He said that we must see the ego as a ghost. He likens the situation to a hiker who believes he sees a snake up the road but discovers upon approaching it that it is a rope. Similarly, the ego appears to be solid until we look at it and see that it is really illusory.

When we first have a thought, it is an "I" thought, and the "I" needs objects to exist. If attention is introverted and we just hang on to the "I" thought, we go through that to the "I am," a sense of existing in a nondualistic way.

When thoughts or emotions arise, we ask: "From where do these thoughts or emotions arise?" Asking this takes us back to the source or the "I-am-ness" of the mind. When teaching Westerners, Ramana Maharshi would quote from the Bible: "I am that I am." This, he said, was the core of his teaching. The quote reflects the state prior to thought, feeling, and the body.

The analogy of a movie may make this clearer. When we go to the movies, we view lots of images on the screen, like the numerous images in the mind when we think. What is real is the screen behind the images—in our mind, this is the emptiness, the consciousness, the beingness from which the images arise.

As long as we devote attention to consciousness instead of content, we are home, liberated, and free. However, the mind always wants to focus on objects. We must practice focusing attention on consciousness rather than transitory objects.

Jack Schwarz describes this process of seeking true identity, beginning with recognizing our true nature. He would ask himself the question, "Who am I?" When he looked up his name in the phone book, the directory listed thirty-five Jack Schwarzes. He realized that Jack Schwarz was just a name and that a more appropriate question to be asking was, "What am I?" From this question he perceived himself as energy, not just a body. Martin Buber, the Jewish philosopher, teaches that what we really are is a part of the universal energy that exists in all living things and which will continue after the body dies. Energy is the transpersonal self, the I-self. Schwarz realized that he could stop telling his body what to do and allow the wisdom of the body, with proper direction of the mind, to tap into the capacity to regenerate cell for cell.

When Schwarz was at the Menninger Foundation demonstrating his ability to put needles in his arm without bleeding, he was often asked how that felt. He replied that he perceived his body as separate from himself and would need to ask his body how it felt, as he was putting a needle not in *his* arm but in *an* arm. He was nonattached to his body, totally beyond the physical structure.[1]

Schwarz's experience doesn't completely explain Ramana Maharshi's teachings, because even describing the self as an energy still keeps the mind focused on an object (although Schwarz comes pretty close).

The technique for practice that Ramana Maharshi gives is continually asking oneself the following:

From where does this thought arise?
Who am I?
To whom does this occur?

Krishnamurti teaches a similar but different approach. He uses observation without a center as a tool for seeing through illusion. It's not one part of thought observing another part of thought. The thinker is the same as the thought, and they can't be separated.

He speaks of observing the movement of thinking or an emotion such as fear. The effect is the content—the thought or emotion becomes insubstantial or unreal. What remains is emptiness and silence.

G. Narayan, who spent a great deal of time with Krishnamurti, explains this sage's work by saying that there is a difference between experience and experiencing. The experience is rooted in the past. Experiencing gathers knowledge and cultivates memories. When we experience something, we stay in the present and our experience is not colored by the past. The experiencer is absent while experiencing.[2]

Attention and observation, or passive awareness, is the tool that enables us to see what is real. It changes the brain cells, transmuting the brain by introducing wholeness.

David Bohm, a quantum physicist, had a very close relationship with Krishnamurti. They had extensive discussions about observation. David Bohm teaches, from a physics point of view, that the observer changes what is being observed. This principle can be compared to Krishnamurti's teaching, in which he states that when a person watches an emotion or mental state as it arises, the emotion or mental state will change on its own, simply through the process of observation.

Ramana Maharshi's and Krishnamurti's approaches are different from typical forms of meditation practices in that the doer or the meditator and thus the ego is eliminated immediately. What remains is wholeness. By contrast, in other forms of meditation the I, the ego, tries to effect change. So if I am angry and want to effect change, this creates conflict. Ramana Maharshi and Krishnamurti do away with the doer, so there is no conflict.

Ramana Maharshi says:

> The attempt to destroy the ego or the mind is just like the thief pretending to be a policeman to catch the thief, that is, himself. Self enquiry alone can reveal the truth that neither the ego nor the mind really exists, and enables one to realise the pure, undifferentiated being of the Self or the Absolute.[3]

Krishnamurti sums up how such a vision of truth can liberate and lead to regeneration:

> When the mind is still, tranquil, not seeking any answer or solution even, neither resisting nor avoiding, it is only then that there can be a regeneration, because then the mind is capable of perceiving what is true and it is the truth that liberates, not our effort to be free.

○ EXERCISES

Before practicing the approaches introduced in this section, read the material several times.

You can work for unlimited times on each practice. First breathe and observe your breathing. As you breathe, be aware of what thoughts, emotions, and sensations arise. Breathing focuses the attention and helps develop concentration. As you observe your breath, you will notice that your breathing slows down. The breath and the mind are connected. When the breath slows down, the mind slows down.

To better understand the reality and source of thought or emotion that arise, ask yourself the following questions repeatedly:

From where does this arise?
Who am I?
To whom does this occur?

To practice observation, simply watch the flow of thought or emotions, and thus the flow of consciousness. Through observation the mind quiets and becomes calmer, and so does the breath.

Both practices will help in the transmutation of negative feelings such as jealousy, anger, loneliness, and fear.

DISIDENTIFICATION

While working toward my master's degree in counseling psychology, I studied psychosynthesis, a potent form of therapy developed by Roberto Assagioli that blends the discoveries of psychoanalysis and the wisdom of spiritual traditions. Assagioli saw psychosynthesis as an attitude whose premise is rooted in the belief that we are already whole and that this wholeness within each of us needs to be recognized.

Assagioli's work in psychosynthesis is filled with many insights I found very valuable in dealing with clients. One of his methods is highly successful for clearing an emotional state and recentering. This exercise, which I use with many clients as well as myself, is easy and extremely powerful in helping us remember who we are.

○ EXERCISES

You might wish to record the following meditation or have someone read it to you as you experience it.

Relax and sit quietly. Look around you and become aware of every detail. Next, close your eyes and inhale slowly, taking inside you vivid visual awareness. Then exhale slowly, asking yourself, "Who is aware?"

With eyes closed, listen to the sounds or the silence around you. Take a deep breath, still listening. Then, as you exhale slowly, ask yourself, "Who listens? Who is aware?"

Still with eyes closed, imagine that you are drawing a circle with chalk on a blackboard. Look at the circle. Then take a deep breath and as you exhale ask yourself, "Who is aware?"

Now let the circle fade away. Continuing to breathe slowly, stay with yourself as the one who is aware. Take time to really experience being yourself.

Repeat the entire exercise several times until you experience the self as the source of stability and clear perception in the midst of change.

Then, with awareness of being your unchanging self, turn your attention to your body. Recognize the changing sensations and conditions of the body over time, in contrast to your unchanging self.

Still aware of being your unchanging self, turn your attention to your feelings. Recognize that your feelings also constantly change, though the self does not change.

Focus again on being your unchanging self. Become aware of your mind, which is always filled with thoughts that change, though the self, the center of awareness, remains unchanged.

Focus again on your unchanging self. Recognize that although the three aspects of body, feelings, and mind are valuable means of expression in the world, they are not you. You have the capacity to direct and regulate the body, feelings, and mind at will.

Experience the following as vividly as possible: "I have a body, but I am not my body. I have emotions, but I am not my emotions. I have a mind, but I am not my mind. I am, rather, that which has a sense of being, permanence, and inner balance. I am a center of identity and pure self-consciousness and will."[4]

To heal the earth through transmutation:

You must be willing to work consciously with the thoughts
you put out as well as the projections being sent to you.
You must not go to war with anything that pollutes you or the
environment. Observing the nature of our world and
experiencing it create transmutation.
You must disidentify with the feelings and thoughts that keep
you from remembering your relationship with life.

Parts of the formula for transmutation used here:

Intention: You must hold an intention to want to work with
the transmutation of negative energy. You must also have a
strong intention to engage in practices that quiet the
emotions and mind.
Love: You can transmute negative energy into energy filled
with love. Energy cannot be destroyed, but it can be
transformed.
Harmony: When you transform negative energy into a healing
energy filled with love, you bring harmony to the planet
and to all life. Remembering that you are not your body,
emotions, or mind will bring you a greater state of
harmony with yourself and others.
Union: When you transmute energy into love, you once again
become merged with your creator. Source created you
from a place of love. Remembering and observing the
unchanging self and your true nature will assist you in
merging with the divine.

Focus: Focus empowers the intention to quiet the mind.

Concentration: To raise your awareness to transmute negative energy on a regular basis takes a great deal of concentration. The key to all meditation practice is concentration.

Imagination: You must be able to imagine negative energy being transmuted into a positive force sent into the universe. You must be able to imagine the possibility that you can quiet your emotions and mind past the illusory nature of the ego.

6

More Tools to Help

RECEIVING

Being able to receive information, healing, and love is a key to being able to transmute energy. We are all looking for love. However, the love that we are seeking is not love that comes from other humans, but divine love. We all suffer from initially attempting to receive this divine love from our parents. Although our bodies were created by our parents, our spirit was created by divine source. Because our parents are egoic in nature, they are not capable of connecting with us on the deep, essential level we crave, but instead project their needs, beliefs, hopes, and fears onto us. Therefore we never feel truly seen or loved by our own parents. We then proceed to evolve different unconscious dysfunctional behaviors in attempts to receive love. For example, we might act out in a relationship, or believe that we can find love by accumulating power, money, or material objects. These are all unhealthy and illusionary paths to receiving the love we truly desire.

In our culture, when we feel unloved by family, friends, authority figures, and significant others, we set up belief systems about why we are unlovable. Such a belief system can be based on psychology; in this regard many of us, in today's society, feel we don't deserve to receive love and nurturance.

Another basis for such a belief system is religion or ethics. For example, through the Christian ethic, we have learned that we must take care of everyone else first before we attend to our own needs, that it is better to give than to receive. However, Angeles Arrien, an anthropologist and teacher of shamanism, believes you cannot learn about giving until you know how to receive, that giving and receiving are all one process. If you are only giving, then you know nothing about giving.

Although we need to bring light into many dark corners of the world and can do this by sharing divine light with others, we cannot give light until we can receive light. This is why it is so important to learn the ability to receive love.

Another reason why learning to receive love is so important is that the current societal imbalance of overgiving coupled with the inability to receive is literally killing us. A study of the profiles of cancer patients reveals that they are people who tend to give too much of themselves to others and don't know how to receive love and nurturance.

In *A Fall to Grace* Lao-tzu says the following to C Alexandra about the importance of nourishment:

> Think of yourself as a growing plant. A plant puts forth beautiful blooms when it has the energy to do so. The more it is fed, the less energy it needs for growth. If at any point your growth requires too much effort, try to find the needed nourishment. This is your responsibility. The river of life will take you to many places, but you must feed yourself along the way.[1]

We all know that all life needs nourishment to grow and heal, but it is not only the body that needs to be nourished. We must learn how to receive love and support from others. For healing to be successful, we must learn how to receive healing energy. We must learn how to receive guidance. And most important, we must learn that it is okay to ask for and accept help.

When working with transmutation, we are asking for assistance from a higher power, whether from source or from compassionate spirits. In response, we might receive the energy needed to transmute, or might be given the guidance we need to do our work. To connect with a higher power, we must be able to receive.

I find that the universe is always there to help us, heal us, and hold us in a place of love. We simply must realize that love and healing are always available to us, and learn how to receive them. Once we project an intention or prayer into the universe, information can come to us in many ways. However, sometimes we are too literal in our expectations and think we will hear some auditory message. Although this can happen, often spiritual information comes as metaphor. Once a call for help or information is put out, it is very possible that the answer the universe provides will come in the form of omens that must be interpreted. The reading of omens is practiced by all indigenous peoples around the world. The most common way of divining information has been the reading of signs presented in nature. You might find, for example, that once you ask for guidance, nature will present you with a sign, such as the appearance of an animal whose qualities will give an answer to your question, or clouds whose forms present a metaphorical response. You might wonder if the omens you receive are an answer to your question or a coincidence. Albert Einstein reminds us that coincidence is God's way of remaining anonymous.

The ability to receive is crucial for raising awareness regarding omens. Noticing omens is not an active, intentional practice but a passive, receptive one. You must state what you are asking from the universe and then surrender to the manner in which information is revealed.

The first time I brought a group to Egypt, I was especially excited about visiting the temple of Isis, as I consider this goddess my teacher. The day before we went, I journeyed to Isis to ask her what gifts we could bring to honor her, and I was very surprised by her response. She said she did not want anyone in the group to bring her gifts. The only gift she wanted was for all of us to receive the healing and love she had to give as we stood in her holy room. This was an example of how gifted it is possible to feel when love is received. Although we don't often give others the gift of receiving their love and support, when we can do this, we set up a sacred space where healing and transformation can occur. We honor the divine when we can receive the nourishment that is provided to us on all levels.

○ E X E R C I S E S

Think about your ability to receive love, support, and healing. Do you take the time to really experience the nurturance that you receive from your food or the universe?

What belief systems or self-talk come up when you look at how you truly feel about being receptive? Write your feelings down. Use some of the techniques discussed previously to help work through these feelings.

Practice being more receptive in your daily life. Notice how life changes for you when you allow yourself to ask for help from others as well as from the power of the universe. Notice how this assistance is always available; we only need to know how to ask for and receive it gracefully. Notice how you feel connected to the people you are in relationship with when you can receive from them.

Practice projecting a call for help and becoming increasingly aware of any omens that are presented by nature or by accidental meetings and conversations with others. For example, occasionally you will encounter someone who, without knowing it, gives you the information you were seeking. Once you can work with omens, you will find yourself in awe of how you are dancing with the mysteries of life. When you become receptive to this process, you will notice that the power of the universe is always presenting you with solutions to your problems.

Try to receive divine information, love, or healing in a dream. There are many ways you can do this. You can ask to receive the divine love of the father in a dream, or the divine love of the feminine, or the unconditional love of the compassionate spirits you work with. You can also ask for a dream to receive healing. You will find that a dream will come if you are persistent in asking every night. By surrendering in your sleep, you might be surprised how the healing or sharing of information or love manifests in metaphors.

PUT SOME ATTENTION ON IT

Sometimes certain issues maintain a hold on us no matter how hard we try to pry into our past to find the source, or engage various healing methods.

However, when nothing else works, focus your attention on the issue. For example, a few years ago I became aware that I did not trust myself. I had always known that I trusted the spirits with whom I have worked for over twenty years, but not myself. I decided that since this issue was blocking my spiritual development, I would work on it. Consequently in my morning meditations and journeys, I asked for help with this issue. I found that the spirits gave me wonderful esoteric solutions that sounded great and made sense, but for me, a human being with an ego, the information was very difficult to put into practice.

For example, the concept of unconditional love for the self is wonderful, but it is hard for the egoic part of oneself to fully integrate this into one's life.

Over the months, I found that on one hand, I really appreciated the insights I was getting from the spirits, while on the other hand, I didn't think it was possible to work with them. However, during this time, I did keep focusing my attention on the issue of trusting myself. Several times a day I would find myself pondering this issue, and after a few months I noticed that I had begun to trust myself. As a result, my journeys for myself and others became stronger, since I didn't have the filter of mistrustful mind chatter.

When I reflected on how this change occurred, I realized it had happened by maintaining attention on the issue. Although I could not come up with any conscious solutions, I retained my awareness that I wanted a change in the trust area, and ultimately it happened.

Next my journeys and meditations made me aware that I had to work on how fear limited me in my work and life. For many years I had explored the past roots of my fear. Once more I found the guidance of the spirits reassuring and beautiful, but a bit too esoteric for practical use. However, again I focused my attention on this issue, and one day I woke up with the absolute resolution that I would not let fear stop me from fully living my life. It was evident to me that I had experienced a real healing.

Through these experiences, it became clear that when conscious practical solutions are not apparent or don't seem to work, we can effect healing and change in our lives by fully putting our attention on issues we want to heal. Light is shed on dark places inside us. Shedding light on an issue is similar to experiencing it and observing it. By raising awareness, you bring the light necessary to transmute the situation. Light and love always heal.

○ E X E R C I S E S

After trying some of the the suggestions for working with issues given in this chapter, if an issue is stubbornly hanging on, put your attention on it. Bring light to the problem. Throughout the day keep decreeing that you want this issue in your life to be resolved. Think about this a few times a day. Don't give up. Keep attending to your decree that you want a healing on the issue you feel stuck with. Stay with it every day until you notice that transmutation has occurred.

As the *I Ching,* the Taoist book of wisdom, teaches, "Perseverance furthers."[2]

To heal the earth through transmutation:

You must first be able to receive the blessings of the divine as well as open to receive divine light which is the force behind all healing.
You can shed light on any problem by putting your attention on it.

Parts of the formula for transmutation used here:

Intention: You must set your intention to receive the energy and love that can transmute pain, illness, and toxins. You must put out a call to receive omens that contain the guidance you are seeking. You must keep your intention strong on the issue you want healed.
Love: Receiving is an act of love. Whenever you decree you want healing, this is a statement of loving yourself.
Harmony: Receiving the gift of love brings harmony into your life. In shedding light on a stubborn problem, you are requesting that harmony return to your life.
Union: Love is a state of union. When you can receive love, you can know union. When you receive omens, you know you are in union and harmony with the flow of life.

To feel connection in your relationships, you must be able to receive.

Focus: You must focus your attention on receiving. Focus brings light to any problem.

Concentration: Concentrate on your ability to receive. Attention requires concentration.

Imagination: To receive love, you must imagine yourself as deserving of love. You must be able to imagine and stay true to your belief in a positive outcome.

III

Love and Imagination

Imagine that you are sitting in a circle with a roomful of people. You close your eyes. You are sitting on the floor and feel the hard wood beneath you. There are many windows in the room, and your senses are alive to what is going on outside the room as well. You are aware of the sun shining down outside, empowering all of life to grow and thrive. You can imagine the celebration of the plant life being nurtured by the sun. You hear the gentle winds going through the trees and the room. And you can smell the sweet scents of nature around you as well as feel the air on your skin.

Inside the room you can hear the sound of your breath in addition to the breathing of those sitting beside you. You can feel the power and energy created by this circle of people. You feel love for yourself as well as for everyone in this circle. You also know that what everyone else feels is love for themselves and for you.

The hair stands up on your skin with the excitement of knowing that from the power, support, and love of the circle a vortex has been created that allows a miracle to take place. Imagine.

Creating Sacred Space

Love heals.

A UNIVERSAL TRUTH

One of the missing pieces to all healing today is understanding the power of creating sacred space. Creating sacred space, as I refer to it here, means the vast energy created by people's individual energies joining together in a room. Today many people create sacred space by actually designing a room, an office, or a house in such a way that allows more energy, vitality, and soul to inhabit that space, but this is not what I am speaking of here.

Over my years of teaching I have noticed what happens when I create a strong container for the group. Miracles! Why? Because everyone in the group can feel safe in opening up to the power of love. Here is a definition of power that I like to use in my work: Power is the ability to use energy.

When everyone in a room is focused on using their energy to support, love, and heal others, that is exactly what occurs, and this is the energy that supports miracles.

In April 1998 I cofacilitated a spiritual journey to Egypt, a very important trip for me, since for the last fourteen years the Egyptian goddess Isis has been my spiritual teacher. It was during a vision quest in 1986 in northern New Mexico that I met Isis, who told me she was returning to the planet at this time to bring love, beauty, and harmony. Consequently, when I finally had the opportunity to visit Isis's home, I was very excited.

The story of Isis and Osiris is the most prevalent spiritual myth in Egypt and one of the world's great love stories. Although there are many versions to this story, the following is a summary of the key events, which express how the miraculous is born from the union of spirits.

Nut, the goddess of the sky, and Geb, the god of the earth, gave birth to Osiris, Set, Horus, Isis, and Nepthys. Set married Nepthys, and Osiris married Isis. Osiris became the great king of Egypt. The people loved him, and he brought great knowledge about agriculture and education to them.

As a result, Set, Osiris's brother, was terribly jealous of him. Ultimately his rageful jealousy led him to kill Osiris, cutting his body into fourteen pieces and scattering them across Egypt.

Isis lamented the news that her husband and true soul mate was now dead. Osiris's sister Nepthys, who also loved him dearly, grieved with Isis, both despairing at the loss of such a love and such a great man.

Because Isis could not leave Osiris scattered across the land, she set out on a long and arduous journey to gather the pieces of her beloved. Though her wandering lasted for many years and she had many adventures, challenges, and tests along the way, she was finally successful. She remembered Osiris by putting his pieces back together and mating with him one last time, conceiving Horus, who eventually avenged his father's death.[1]

Numerous Egyptian spiritual teachings revolve around this myth, and as our group journeyed from temple to temple we saw depictions of the story of Isis and Osiris on the walls. One day we came to the temple of the pharaoh Seti I at Abydos, where it is believed the head of Osiris was found. There we saw a wall with pictographs, one of which depicted Osiris lying dead on a cement slab and Isis in her spiritual form of a bird mating with him.

In interpreting the image, our guide explained that Isis could not do a soul retrieval for Osiris in her human form, for in this form, she could not remember him. She had to take her spiritual form to remember him and mate with him to conceive Horus.

This statement had a profound impact on me, but it was not until I left Egypt and had time to reflect that I began to realize the true meaning of what I had experienced. What I understood was that the magical birth of Horus occurred through the merging of Isis and Osiris in spirit; that is, the union of spirit created a magical being, the holy child.

As a result of this intriguing revelation, I began considering aspects of other traditions that expressed the similar idea. For example in Matthew 18:20 Jesus Christ says: "When two or three are gathered in my name, I am among you."

What this really means is that from the union of spirits, something holy, something magical, is born.

In the practice of cross-cultural shamanic healing it is well known that the power of the healing for an individual or for a piece of land is multiplied exponentially by the number of compassionate family, friends, and community members present at the healing. This occurs because the community present agrees to put their personality and egos aside, allowing for a greater spiritual energy to be called forth and gather for the healing work.

Through study and experience, I realized that what these spiritual teachings mean is that when two or more spiritual energies come together, the union generates a third energy that, if correctly focused, can be what I and others call the magical child—the energy of change, transformation, and healing.

Unfortunately, what usually happens when a group of people come together in our culture is that they focus on their feelings of alienation and on individual concerns. They look around the room to assess their competitors or determine whom they feel most threatened by.

Often when I teach long residential workshops, there is at least one person who tells me that he feels separate and alienated from the group. I am always hearing these words: "I don't feel like I fit in. I don't know where my place is. Everyone in the group seems to be in harmony with each other, and I feel outside of what is happening." What usually surprises me in such circumstances is that the person who claims this is often the most extroverted one in the group. If this individual is feeling isolated, what is everyone else experiencing?

When we are in touch with the spiritual side of ourselves, we feel in harmony and in union with all of life. However, when we are in our egoic state, we feel separate. This reflects our original fall from grace, when we separated from the source of life and from each other. Even though it is characteristic of the human condition to feel such separateness, it is not conducive to creating energy for healing and transmutation.

However, imagine if the opposite was true. Imagine what would happen if we had compassion for the human side of ourselves and were thus able to leave that part of ourselves behind and get in touch with our spiritual side, which knows that the feeling of separation is pure illusion. Then we would make a conscious decision to open up our hearts to ourselves and others without feelings of competitiveness, jealousy, or alienation, knowing that we all want love, to be healed, and to live our lives in harmony. As a result, a third energy would be born that would produce transmutation. A door would then open, allowing the miracle of love and healing to enter.

Every time you are in the presence of other individuals, your energy merges with them in union to create a new energy. We are constantly conceiving a divine child through divine means without realizing it. This is what I call creating sacred space.

In our culture, we focus on the process of individuation. We have learned how to find what we want and to set boundaries with family, friends, and coworkers. This has been very significant work, as we need to have a better sense of self. But it's also important to realize that from a spiritual perspective, boundaries do not exist.

Certainly we can set emotional boundaries between ourselves and others and learn to distinguish the difference between our emotions and those of others, so we do not become burdened by their feelings. However, the truth is that energy cannot be contained. Energy flows out from us all the time.

Often we are unconscious about the energies we release when we are in an emotional state. For example, when someone walks into a room filled with anger, the feeling is tangible. When someone walks into a room filled with love, that feeling is also tangible. We have no energetic boundaries; we are constantly merging our energies with others. If you have ever been at a religious, spiritual, political, or celebratory gathering where people sing together, you have felt the palpable experience of energy in the room. Such energy has definite healing and empowering qualities.

Once when I shared my thoughts about this phenomena with a nun, her response summed up the power of the process: "In a way, that's the idea of mass and other religious rituals, but in some way all that has become too routine and too institutionalized. The whole contemplative thrust is about creating sacred space—emptying one-self of ego concerns and lower-vibrational-level elements—so that one can truly encounter and engage with the divine energy. In this process, transformation or transmutation can occur."

A few years ago Catholic Health Services asked me to give a keynote lecture at a conference on the topic of how to bring shamanism into the Catholic health-care system. I gave a very frank, clear lecture on how shamans around the world perceive illness and the spiritual healing methods used. I spoke about how these spiritual healing methods could be applied to modern culture.

I was apprehensive about this lecture, since the average age of the priests and nuns in the audience was sixty, and I did not know how open they would be to hearing about shamanism and journeying to helping spirits. Consequently, the night before my talk I meditated. The message I received was to visualize and experience myself merging with Our Lady of Guadalupe, a saint that I have meditated on for years, before I began to speak.

As a result, the response to my lecture was very good, which delighted but shocked me. Most noteworthy was the fact that many of the nuns came up to me afterward and said that they hadn't focused so much on my words but instead were mesmerized by the love and peace of some spiritual force around me, the result of speaking so passionately about my shamanic work and being merged with Our Lady of Guadalupe. From this experience I learned how union and love can create a healing and divine space where words become insignificant but the power of the energy becomes transformative.

Imagine what could happen if you walked into the office of a doctor, psychotherapist, or other healer and both of you focused your heart and spiritual energies to create healing energy. In our quest for sources of healing, we are missing a key resource. It is time to incorporate in our lives and work the knowledge of creating sacred space, a space in which true transmutation can occur. Techniques don't heal; love heals.

O Exercises

The following is a simple exercise to invoke the feeling of creating sacred space. Every day for one week light a candle in a room, for as little as a few minutes or as much as an hour. For many people, burning candles signifies celebratory or sacred occasions. We often light candles at special meals, for relaxation when taking a bath, or at religious sites. Candles usually signify bringing forth a special energy. They signify the power of light. Notice how you feel when you are in a room with a glowing candle. Do you notice something special? Do you feel a sweet, gentle energy permeating your space? This energy is an example of what creating sacred space feels like. Remember how it feels.

Here is another exercise.

When you are in a room with several people, look around you. (Start off with something simple. Don't first try this while you are in a movie theater or at a concert. Start in your workplace, at a group meeting, or with friends. Let's begin with the basics before you take on the world.) Notice how you are feeling. Notice any feelings of being threatened, not good enough, or separate that might be coming up. Just notice these feelings. Don't fight them. In Taoist psychology the only way to transform an energy is by meeting it completely and not resisting it. Have compassion for yourself and recognize that this is just one part of you, your ego, having these feelings. Realize that everyone on this planet, unless enlightened, has these same feelings.

Now take a few deep breaths. Use your breathing to bring you to a centered place. With your breath, start to change your consciousness and your awareness. Remember that because we are all human, we all have fragilities and we all have been wounded. Have compassion for each person in the room who acts from a place of woundedness instead of love. Make a conscious decision to contact your spiritual side and embrace each person in the room with love.

Then ask yourself the following questions to gain a greater understanding of the qualities of sacred space: How does the energy in the room change? How does your behavior change? How do your feelings change for humankind? Did the power of healing, love, and transmutation enter the room by your focused intention and attention?

What distractions keep you from creating sacred space? Do you find yourself distracted by negative thoughts? Do you feel as though there is not enough time? Does mental chatter inhibit you?

Remember, life is a spiritual practice. This has to be done every day in order to perceive long-term results. It takes discipline, focus, and intention. Make a commitment to yourself to slow down when you relate in a group, and instead of reacting, bring the energy of love into your life and the lives of others.

To heal the earth through transmutation, you must be willing to call forth your divinity and join together with your community to birth the holy, divine energy that transmutes your environment.

Parts of the formula for transmutation used here:

Intention: You must have a clear intention to put aside your egoic feelings of separation to use your spiritual energy to create healing and transformation in sacred space.

Love: You must love yourself, other people, and all living beings to invoke divine energy.

Harmony: You must harmonize your energy with your spiritual side and the spiritual energy of others.

Union: When you allow your spiritual energy to merge with the spiritual energy of others, you create the divine child. This third energy can create transmutation.

Focus: It takes focused intention to transform energy in a group.

Concentration: You must concentrate your efforts on holding your intention to bring love, harmony, and union into your environment.

Imagination: You must invoke your imagination to believe that you can really be part of creating a healing space.

8

Imagination

In my dream,
the angel shrugged
and said if we fail this
time it will be a
failure of imagination

and then she
placed the world
gently in the palm of my hand

Imagination is another important resource for healing and trans-mutation. I have always had a very vivid imagination, which has made my life rich, but when I work with clients or students and observe people around me, I notice frequently that many are out of touch with imagination. This is unfortunate, since our imagination is a key ingredient in healing, changing our lives, and working with transmutation. I cannot stress enough the power of this incredible resource.

As I discussed in Chapter 4, when a person loses his soul, he loses pure essence or life force. During a soul retrieval that is what is brought back, and it is possible for the practitioner to see details about why that pure essence was lost. However, unless the practi-tioner uses the right words to explain the journey, the client feels that trauma was returned instead of pure essence. Clients often become stuck in the words, and their imaginations are not stimulated to heal.

For example, I journey for someone shamanically and am shown that a young child lost a piece of his soul because of intense fear while watching his parents have a terrible fight. What is being shown is why the pure essence left at this time. What is being brought back is life force, vitality, and pure essence. But if I am not careful with my words, the client will believe I brought back a fearful child. The results will be easy to predict in this case: The client will now be overwhelmed with fear.

The metaphor that I use to express this in my healing work and teaching is planting seeds. Every time we speak words to people we are planting seeds. The question is, are we planting seeds of fear or are we planting seeds of hope?

Shamans all over the world have been psychologists as well as spiritual healers and advisors in their communities. They have always used healing words and stories in their practices. Shamans told stories that they knew would heal the clients and the communities. In Part V, we will look at how words were used to heal and create.

By contrast, Larry Dossey, author and lecturer on the mind-body connection and the power of prayer, has shown in our culture how doctors often use words that cause their patients distress. Citing examples in his books *Meaning and Medicine* and *Be Careful What You Pray For,* he has been very courageous in demonstrating how the use of words can be devastating to people and how words can hurt instead of heal.

He relates a story of a fifty-one-year-old schoolteacher who had undergone surgery for cancer. She responded well to the surgery and had plans for a bright future. The night before she was scheduled to be discharged from the hospital, her doctor told her that there were other tumors in her body that could not be removed. He told her she had six to twelve months to live. As a result, the woman fell into a depression and died three days later.[1]

In modern-day psychology and medicine we often focus on what is wrong, planting seeds of problems that seem to then be perpetuated. When we are told how to deal with our problems, instead of allowing our own self-determination and creativity to heal us, our creative genius is denied, with oftentimes devastating consequences.

In one of my workshops a doctor told a wonderful story that illustrates this point. A man went to his doctor for a checkup. The doctor told him that he had cancer and had about six months to live. The man, showing no emotion, left the office, and the doctor did not see him again. Many years went by, and the doctor was doing some work at a hospital when the same patient showed up there. In disbelief, the doctor told himself, "This is impossible. The man should have died years ago." As it turned out, the man had not been wearing his hearing aid when the doctor initially told him that he had cancer. The rest I will leave to your imagination.

Imagination is a God-given gift. We can use our imagination to heal and transmute, or we can utilize it to create illness and trauma. In saying this, I am not suggesting that we are entirely responsible for our illnesses. Pollutions do exist that affect our bodies, and often illness is the only way we can get rid of toxins. Moreover, illness is sometimes a means of getting us to assess our lives.

In his novel *Sphere,* Michael Crichton brilliantly describes the power and uniqueness of the human imagination.

> On your planet you have an animal called a bear. It is a large animal, sometimes larger than you, and it is clever and has ingenuity, and it has a brain as large as yours. But the bear differs from you in one important way. It cannot perform the activity you call imagining. It cannot make mental images of how reality might be. It cannot envision what you call the past and what you call the future. This special ability of imagination is what has made your species as great as it is. Nothing else. It is not your ape-nature, not your tool-using nature, not language or your violence or your caring for

young or your social groupings. It is none of these things, which are all found in other animals. Your greatness lies in imagination.

He goes on to say that what we call intelligence is mostly our imagination. We don't always acknowledge that it is our imagination that makes things happen. As we are unaware of this great power we contain, we do not control our imaginings. We imagine wonderful things as well as terrible things and do not take responsibility for the choice. We say we have both the power of good and evil inside of us, but in truth what we do have is the ability to imagine.[2]

The Reverend Eloise Page, a well-known eighty-eight-year-old psychic medium, also stresses the power of imagination: "Fantasy is what many describe as imaginary or illusionary or wishful thinking. Imagination or the power of creativity are very real and concrete forces, they are neither imaginary, nor illusions."[3]

Neville, a twentieth-century mystic and teacher, wrote numerous books on the power of imagination in the 1940s that echo my theories on the use of imagination. For example, Neville succinctly describes the power of the imagination on our lives in the following statement: "Our future is our own imaginal activity in its creative march."[4] He adds, "All imaginative men and women are forever casting forth enchantments, and all passive men and women, who have no powerful imaginative lives, are continually passing under the spell of their power."[5]

What Neville stresses in his lectures and writings is that we must see what we desire from the endpoint. It is not enough to desire or visualize what we want; we must imagine the scene as if it has already happened. He adds to this other components that he found essential for working with the imagination to bring positive results.

Neville instructs us to see the world as clay and our imagination as the potter. Using our gift of imagination, we must faithfully shape the end we desire.[6]

We often block our creative potential by rationalizing what we can't do by stating facts. But facts, as we perceive them, are once again creations of imagination. If we change what we imagine, we will change the facts.[7]

Neville also talks about the importance of understanding our oneness with God and divine forces as our imagination seeks something deeper and more fundamental than just creating things. In reality, what we do is actually what God is doing in and through man, who is imagination.[8]

Caroline Casey, astrologer, author, and lecturer, also vividly expresses a similar idea: "Imagination lays the tracks for the reality train to follow."[9] Sit with this line for a while and let it sink in. This statement holds great power.

We are dreaming our world into existence all the time. What we don't realize is that by not taking an active role in visioning our lives, we end up manifesting chaos from our confused and troubled thoughts. The source of life manifested creation from a deep still and silent place. We must be able not only to reawaken our ability to imagine a good life, but to create a peaceful, still, and silent place to manifest from.

Part of being able to fully use our imagination for transmutation involves getting in touch with all our senses. It is not enough just to see a scene. We need to be able to touch, hear, smell, and taste the scene we are visualizing.

When I was in Egypt I got a lesson in the importance of using the imagination to vividly experience scenes. I had time to meditate in front of a great statue of the lion-headed goddess, Sekhmet, in the temple of Karnak. Her advice to me was to taste life—advice that surprised me, since I had not thought of experiencing life in terms of taste. As a result of this encounter, I realized that taste had been a sense I had excluded in my daily life and in my spiritual work. To work with this, I had to look at what the metaphor of tasting the world meant, concluding that it meant taking life into my being completely and using my imagination to effect transformation.

The power of our imagination and of actively opening ourselves to life's flow has been emphasized and well documented. However, some interesting research on the power of prayer has also been done. Larry Dossey, who has studied the effects of prayer on healing, concludes that more healing takes place when people use the prayer "Thy will be done" instead of praying for a specific result.

At first it might seem that the principles of being active and using imagination to effect healing and using such a nonspecific prayer to achieve the same effect contradict each other. However, they are both imperative principles in connection with healing ourselves and the planet.

In the practice of shamanism, the shaman actively seeks a result but also works in partnership with helping spirits. This means that the shaman brings healing power from the spirits but also takes action himself. These principles are not opposed in shamanism.

Similarly, in her book *The Passion of Isis and Osiris,* Jean Houston says that ancient Egyptian initiates were trained to effect transmutation through a combination of personal and divine power: "The ability to transform by desire and by alignment of the will with the divine was the revelation of the higher level initiates."[10]

I have observed people give all responsibility in life over to the divine, taking no action and believing the universe would bring everything necessary to them. This experiment failed, which I believe underscores the need for balance between acknowledging divine power and accepting responsibility for our growth and transmutations. Yes, we want to pray for divine will to be done; it's important to align ourselves with a higher power. But the bottom line is that our thoughts are constantly creating much of what we perceive and ultimately become.

What we believe we also experience. What happens for many people when they begin to work with visualizations and realizing desires is that they are completely unaware of how their unconscious beliefs control the outcome. For example, if you work on creating a healthy body but deep down don't believe you can actually do it, your goal will be sabotaged by that negative self-talk, and the work will not be successful. Our inner conversations do have an effect on what we manifest in our lives.

All spiritual traditions speak to the relationship between the microcosm and macrocosm. I have already discussed how the phrase "As above, so below; as within, so without" is the basis of all metaphysics. When I wrote the visionary fiction work *A Fall to Grace,* the underlying theme became "In and out are the same." This means the outer world always reflects back to us what is happening in our own inner state. If we want to change our external world, we must first change our internal world.

This poem from Browning expresses the importance of knowing that what is within us is manifested outside us:

> *Truth is within ourselves; it*
> *takes no rise*
> *From outward things, what e'er*
> *you may believe*
> *There is an inmost center in us*
> *all,*
> *Where truth abides in fullness*
> *. . . and to know,*
> *Rather consist in opening out a*
> *way*
> *Whence the imprisoned splendor*
> *may escape,*
> *Then in effecting entry for a*
> *light*
> *Supposed to be without.*[11]

I have written *Medicine for the Earth* for those of you who are seeking a better life by seeking a true spiritual path. I am attempting to teach a very powerful means for people to heal themselves, others, and the planet, rather than trying to show how to use spiritual principles to gain material objects and wealth or to manipulate the universe to achieve power over others.

I am addressing people who have discovered that material objects or wealth do not create happiness and who instead are seeking food for their souls by finding true meaning in life and bringing passion and creativity into their daily lives.

In writing about the power of the imagination, I am asking people to reach for their highest potential and use their imagination to create better conditions for healing life on the planet. We need to imagine a planet with clean air to breathe and clean water to drink, not how to buy a new expensive car. It is fine to use your imagination to manifest material things, but it will anchor you to here, preventing you from experiencing the divine union necessary to heal ourselves and transmute environmental pollution.

To do this, we must change our consciousness and examine the difference between using our imagination to serve small, egoic desires and utilizing it to serve our highest potential and humanity.

To align with what is for the highest good for ourselves and the planet, we use our own imaginative creative energies along with asking, "Thy will be done." In this way we partner with the power of the universe and avoid making the mistake of thinking our own ego knows what is best for all concerned.

There are specific traps to watch out for in working with creative powers. As you work more with your imagination and creative powers, you can avoid being trapped by egoic desires through aligning your own vision with the spiritual powers of the universe. In this way you work in harmony with the powers that be and avoid accidentally misusing your power. Further, in working on your own spirituality and use of spiritual power, you must simultaneously examine your own emotional state and psychological development so that you do not use your spiritual gifts and knowledge in a negative manner. The well-known black magician Aleister Crowley (1875–1947), for example, had a clear understanding of the connection between the microcosm and the macrocosm but used his understanding and knowledge for only selfish purposes and to control others around him. Aleister Crowley paid quite the price for this, living a miserable life and suffering a terrible death.

I am on a path to bring heaven to earth. To accomplish this goal, I encourage everyone to use spiritual methods that create the miracles to heal all beings on the earth, and to always reach for your highest potential. This is what will feed your soul and will create the happiness you are looking for. There is no greater food for the soul than to benefit all of life. Imagine if we all gathered our spiritual forces together to heal our communities and environment.

The dilemma of knowing when to ask "Thy will be done" and when to use our active imagination comes down to who is making the decision. The confusion usually occurs when it is our ego talking. If you find yourself pursuing material goals, then your ego is making the choices, and to avoid problems you might be better off requesting, "Thy will be done."

There is another aspect of the issue of creating from an egoic state that must be addressed. We are part of the whole and therefore not separate from the forces of nature. You can create what you believe, but you must also acknowledge and work in harmony with the laws of nature. In Part IV we will see how we do not have power over nature, and for your transmutation work to be successful, you must be in alignment with the power of the universe. The key is harmony with yourself as well as with spiritual and natural forces when using your imagination to create.

Part of our fall from grace is feeling separate from source, while the other part is feeling separate from our spirit. When we ask our spirit to say what it wants, the answer will always involve love. It only requests acts of kindness and love.

In *Welcome Home: Following Your Soul's Journey Home,* I describe a spiritual teaching I once received from Isis about discovering joy in life:

> So my advice to you and the people who live around you is to step back from your life. Use your imagination to envision what you would like your life to be like. Try to imagine what joy and happiness feel like. Reach back to at least one experience in which you felt happy. What situations and experiences do you think would help you regain those feelings? Trust yourself and have faith that you can create this feeling again in your life.[12]

As I travel around the world teaching workshops and lecturing, I notice that people have a preoccupation with negative prophecies. However, I believe that the so-called Armageddon is here now and has been for quite some time. We are now experiencing fires, earthquakes, floods, volcanic eruptions, tidal waves, disease, drought, famine, and pestilence. Further, I am curious about why people get so excited when they speak about doom and gloom to come when natural disasters have occurred throughout recorded history.

I believe this is the result of knowing that our lives are empty and lack meaning. We want something to change this. We don't want to take responsibility for making those changes, but instead want something—even a disaster—outside of our control to force our lives to change.

But do we really need tragedy to change? Unfortunately, sometimes learning through tragedy is how human beings grow. While tragedy is not essential for change, when we experience a tragedy in our lives, we value life more; learn the great importance of health and come to appreciate what we have; reprioritize what is important to us; and discover how to live in the present, because that is all we have.

However, many of us focus on negative prophecy because we don't want to take responsibility for changing our lives. Caroline

Casey says, "It is better to create prophecy than to live prediction."[13] As my good friend Coreen says: "What future are we voting for?"

Moreover, in visioning a new future, it's important not only to vision our future as we want it, but also to realize that our future is created by our present. To manifest visions of the future, we must shape and sculpt our present accordingly; we must sow the seeds of the plants we wish to reap.

As I have already stated, shamans around the world have a saying: "We are dreaming the wrong dream." Many spiritual traditions and philosophers view this world as the world of illusion.

I, too, believe that we are all dreaming here. And what we need to learn to do is dream lucidly in our waking state. Let's dream together a pure, clean planet of beauty, where we can live in harmony with ourselves, the rest of life, and nature. Let's all dream about perceiving heaven on earth now.

○ EXERCISES

Look at your life as if it were an artwork created in whatever medium you wish. Become the artist of your life. Step back and focus your attention on what you see. What feelings does your artwork evoke? Pick up your paintbrush, sculpting tool, or other implement corresponding to your chosen medium and make changes that reflect your own desires and place in your evolution of consciousness. All creativity takes great risks. Don't be afraid to make a mistake. There is no right way for your art and life to look, so experiment. You can always rework anything that does not reflect your soul's desires.

Write about a dream you imagine your life to be. Don't put anything into your dream about manifesting money or material objects. Dream on how you want your life to flow, what kind of relationships you want, how you want to use your time, what life priorities are important to you.

Have a visioning party, where those who choose to come tell their personal and global visions. Speaking about these visions publicly, as well as having community support, sets the stage for these creations to take form.

Choose one day for each of your senses—seeing, hearing, touching, smelling, and tasting. Make a conscious decision to go through that day focusing on the appropriate sense. After the five senses are explored separately, take a day and focus on them altogether.

Here's a challenge for you: Watch a night of television and notice what seeds are planted inside you by what you see and hear. Notice what gets stimulated in your imagination. Think about the images you are being fed and their potential effects on your life.

To heal the earth through transmutation, you must be able to dream a clean, pure, and healed earth into being.
Parts of the formula for transmutation used here:

Intention: In using your imagination, it is essential you have a strong intention of what you are calling into your life.
Love: You must love yourself and the planet to create a positive present and future for all of life.
Harmony: You must create from a place of harmony with all life rather than for selfish purposes.
Union: You must merge with your highest self and the power of the universe so that "thy will be done."
Focus: To imagine a world free of pollution takes great focus.
Concentration: Every day you must hold your vision of what you want your future to be, which takes a tremendous amount of concentration. You must concentrate on using

all your senses—seeing, hearing, smelling, touching, and tasting what you want to manifest in the world. You must concentrate on experiencing what you want as if the end result has already manifested.

Imagination: It is up to you to dream a new dream. You need to be able to imagine what you want your future to be.

9

Receiving the Gifts of Our Ancestors

We honor the ancestors who went before us.
We honor the descendants who go after us.
We honor all of life.

Today many people have chosen to work on life problems through psychotherapeutic help. In modern psychology, emphasis is placed on what we did not get from our families, especially our parents. For people who had abusive childhoods, this is often the focus. In doing this valuable work, psychotherapists have helped people learn how to have more functional relationships. But in looking only at what we didn't get from our families, we are missing a very valuable resource in our lives.

If we move from a psychological perspective to a biological perspective, emphasizing survival of the fittest, we see that we would not be here if we had not received gifts from our family—genes adapting us for survival. In the United States, many people do not know their own family origins. We know only our own dysfunctional family history. But tools for survival have been passed down to us. If we don't know our past, then we don't know our future. Having some sense of our ancestral line is imperative for understanding and appreciating the continuum of life.

For years I have been trying to find out about my family history. I long to know who my ancestors were, how they struggled, and what gifts helped them survive. On my mother's side of the family, everyone I quizzed recalled stories that directly conflicted with each other. For example, my mother remembers hearing from her parents that communication ended with relatives who stayed in Russia because of persecution of those receiving letters from the United States. My uncle says that no, they just wanted to stop writing.

My father thinks his family came from Russia but just isn't sure. None of his family knows. My family on both sides let go of their past and integrated as quickly as possible into the American culture.

Although I know my spiritual roots with the divine, I have felt a hole inside not being able to tap into the richness of my own family history. I can only imagine the wealth of stories that have been lost, and how they could only have added to my understanding of the strengths I have today and my future possibilities.

When I turned to my spiritual practice to enlighten me, I found that my own shamanic gifts had been passed down through my mother's family. This knowledge provided me with a frame of reference for all I had truly received from my own mother. In a journey on this issue, I had a wonderful image of a great-great-great-grandmother in the Ukraine who looked just like me, dancing in ceremony with her arms reaching toward the sky. It left me with a great appreciation for what all my ancestors went through and how I have benefited from their lives.

We have looked at the significance of being in union with spirit, the spirits, and the gods and goddesses. We have learned that we are born from divine source rather than through our parents. Now it is time to look at what spiritual, emotional, and physical gifts were passed down through our own biological ancestry. This work is especially important for people who have been abused by their families. Looking at this aspect will provide you with great healing, once you feel you are ready to proceed with this.

Think about your family members. What are some of the good traits you see in yourself that are also reflected in other family members? If one of your parents or grandparents is especially intuitive or psychic, do you have this gift? Do any of your family members have a sense of humor like you? Are you carrying on any qualities of persistence? What about spiritual, emotional, or physical strengths? Are you carrying out any of your family talents, such as being creative through writing, dancing, singing, art?

When you reach inside yourself, what family traits are you proud of embodying? Let go of any judgments about what your family may have done or not done with these gifts. Your choices concerning how to use your talents may be different from other family members' choices. We live in a time when we can express our souls, something that was not always true for preceding generations.

WHO ARE OUR TEACHERS?

Our greatest teachers are the people who inspire and empower us. There's an old Zen saying: "If you meet the Buddha on the road, kill him." This means that anyone claiming to know more than you is not your teacher. Creation and inspiration come from deep inside, not from an external source. Go deep inside and create; birth yourself from the inside out.

Jean Houston quotes the mystical writer Meister Eckhart, who imagines God speaking to us about our own potential: "I became man for you. If you do not become God for me, you do me wrong."[1] Also in this context, the words of my dream, quoted earlier on page 45, are relevant: "Man has been looking for God outside of himself for the last two thousand years. Man will be looking for God inside of himself for the next two thousand years."

We are all creative geniuses, every one of us. It is time to recognize this truth. It is also important to acknowledge that all of us must be responsible for transmuting the poisons around us. This is not just the task of a few individuals, nor can anyone else transmute the pain and illnesses in you. Only you can do this by recognizing the powerful being that you are and focusing your attention on your desired goals.

There is not only one technique that will work. And although stories from those who have been in touch with their abilities may be inspirational, you will need to find your own way. We need to stop relying of the authority of others and recognize our own gifts and strengths as well as see ourselves as equals with others. If you choose to study with others, focus on the teachings, not the person transmitting the knowledge.

A statement by the Indian guru Ramakrishna about Western people relayed by Ken Cohen, a writer on chi gong, reflects the tendency of most people to continue searching for teachers they believe will lead the way: We begin to dig a well, but we do not stay with the digging in order to find water. We just keep digging new wells. I observe people all over the world go from workshop to workshop thinking that some new teacher holds the magic key, but the truth is that each one of us is the holder of this key.

O E X E R C I S E S

Make a list of people you give your power away to because you think they have more knowledge and authority than you.

What is being reflected and mirrored back to you about your own abilities? If you can see power and knowledge in someone else, then you must also possess such power and knowledge.

To heal the earth through transmutation:

You must appreciate and focus on the gifts, strengths, and
possibilities you carry through your ancestral line.
You must have faith in your potential and power to perform
the healing work needed to be done.

Parts of the formula for transmutation used here:

Intention: You must hold the intention to look past the flaws
of your family to acknowledge the gifts you received from
them and own your power.
Love: Behind fear and anger there is always love. Your own
family had love for you. You must love and honor the
teacher inside of you.
Harmony: Looking at the skills being passed down to you
through your ancestry puts you in harmony with
your past. When you recognize that you are a powerful
being who can create change, you harmonize with
yourself, thereby harmonizing with the power of the
universe.
Union: The skills passed down to you create union with a
genetic line that knows how to survive.
Focus: You must focus on the gifts you have received from
your ancestors as well as your ability and potential to
transmute pollution.
Concentration: You must concentrate on using the talents
passed down to you instead of rejecting them because of

the source. You must concentrate on the spiritual practices needed to help you embrace your own knowing.

Imagination: You must use your imagination to see past the flaws of your ancestors and tap into their gifts, as well as imagine that you are connected to source.

IV

Harmony with Nature Within and Without

Imagine going to your favorite place in nature, a place that brings you peace and healing. Close your eyes and take a few deep breaths. In your mind's eye imagine being in this place as fully as you can at this point in time. With your eyes closed, experience the beauty and peacefulness of this place. Look around you and see all that there is to see there. What plant life is there with you? Are there any animals around? Are there rocks here? Is there any water here? What does the earth look like? What colors are surrounding you? Is the sun out? What is the quality of the sky? Is it daytime or nighttime?

Now feel yourself being in this place. Feel the air on your skin. Is it warm or is it cool? Is the quality of the air dry or wet? Is the air still or is there a wind? What does the earth feel like beneath your feet? Touch the earth with your hands. What does it feel like?

What are the sounds of nature? Do you hear any wind, animal noises, or sounds of running water?

Smell all the fresh smells of the life around you. What are you smelling now?

Open up all your senses to this place and take it in as fully as you can. Feel your energy expand. Experience your mind quieting. Experience the peace and healing of this place. Feel what it feels like to be in harmony with yourself and the natural world. Remember your connection with all living beings in this place. You are not here alone. You are part of a greater whole.

Imagine your favorite tree being in this place. Look around you and find it. Experience yourself walking up to it and with your heart ask if it is okay if you sit by it. Experience the answer in your heart.

As you sit with this tree breathe deeply. As you breathe deeper and deeper allow your consciousness to merge with the consciousness of the tree. Allow your body to become one and merge with the tree.

Experience what it is like to be a tree. Allow your roots to run deep into the earth receiving fully the nurturance the earth generously offers you. Imagine your branches reaching toward the sun, collecting the energy of the sun, growing toward the light.

You are now the tree of life. Experience yourself bridging heaven and earth through your trunk, your body. Allow yourself as much time in meditation as you need to experience being this tree.

When you are ready, through intention, separate your consciousness from this tree. Thank the tree for letting you merge with it. Remember the feelings of having deep roots receiving nurturance and having branches which collect the power of the sun. Remember what it is like to be a bridge between heaven and earth. With these memories, allow your consciousness to drift slowly back to the room and to your body.

10

Reconnecting with Nature

Humankind has not woven the web of life. We are but one
thread within it. Whatever we do to the web, we do to
ourselves. All things are bound together. All things connect.
— ATTRIBUTED TO CHIEF SEATTLE

Harmony is one of the key elements to our formula for transmutation. In order for transmutation of personal and environmental illness to occur, we must be in harmony with nature.

As you read in the introduction, my true purpose in writing this book is to bring back ancient wisdom to help us in transmuting environmental pollution. As we became disconnected from spirit and our own divinity, we became more and more disconnected from other living beings and from nature. This disconnection has created most of the toxins and pollutions we now need to transmute in order to survive.

In all of my previous books I have written about the importance of connecting with nature for true healing to take place. Connecting with the earth's rhythms and cycles is also important as we look at transmutation. We can't transmute environmental pollution until we once again understand our connection with nature, the cycles of the moon, the seasons, the elements, and all of life. Harmony with the earth's cycles and the forces of nature is essential, since disconnection and disharmony with nature create disease.

I notice in my travels that I meet more and more people with thyroid problems. The thyroid is a part of us that is affected by environmental toxins. I am also meeting more and more people suffering from allergies and environmental illness.

Many individuals who face these kinds of environmental illnesses and sensitivities feel that they have become weak. However, it's a misperception to consider these illnesses as weakness. These particular illnesses and allergies are the sign of an intelligent body, not a weak body. The body is saying, "Something is wrong here, something is out of balance, something is polluted."

Today it is well understood that stress has a negative impact on our physical bodies and our emotional health. But we do not yet recognize the tremendous stress caused by not following nature's cycles, nor that this also leads to emotional and physical illness. Just imagine the physical stress of walking against the flow of a rushing river. This is what we do spiritually as we walk against the flow of the river of life on a daily basis. Imagine trying to stop the flow of a river. All of life and nature is in continual motion—the moon, the sun, plant growth, cell growth. We must learn to bend in response to the natural forces that are moving us, just as the river, the stars, the moon, the sun, and the wind do. Any attempt to halt the natural rhythm of life will lead to a path of disharmony.

Our bodies are intelligent; it is our egos that are weak and ill. Our egos live under the delusion that not only can we separate ourselves from nature, but we are in control of nature.

This belief is not just wrong; in fact, it is killing us. Cancer is prevalent today among people of all ages. Instead of looking at how to kill the cancer, why don't we put our attention and intention to examining what is causing the cancer? Our bodies tell us something is wrong, but we ignore them. We can no longer live our lives from such a deluded place.

Nature presents the cure for our illnesses in giving us the plant life to heal us. Scientists have discovered what shamans have known for

thousands of years: There is a plant that can cure every illness presented to humankind. Yet we go destroy the forests these plants grow in. Science tells us that we can replicate the active substances of these plants in a laboratory and don't need the live plant itself.

Let's ponder this for a moment. Sit inside yourself and close your eyes. Bring into your awareness the words "artificial life" and "life from light." Which of those sets of words has more energy behind it? Of "artificial and synthetic" or "life with light," which of these would you want to ingest, adding its life force to your body? Ask your intelligent body to make the decision here. What does your body tell you?

How did we lose our sense of harmony with the environment? One obvious way is that as we became technologically advanced we thought we didn't need to be in deep connection with nature. We have houses with cooling and heating systems that protect us from the extremes of environment. We have stores to buy our food in. We have clocks and calendars by which we can tell time and the change in seasons.

Our perceived obligations have skewed our priorities of what is important. We tend to live very fast-paced and stressful lives, rather than taking time to be in union with nature. There can be no transmutation without union. There's more than the creator to be in union with. We must reconnect with nature to fully understand the web of life.

By disconnecting ourselves from nature and the earth, the bigger body we live in, we became more and more disconnected from ourselves. As we look at harmonizing with nature, we must look at harmonizing with ourselves. This is all part of the web of life. This is why so much of *Medicine for the Earth* has been devoted to healing our inner world. Our inner world has a profound effect on our outer world. Healing where we are out of harmony with the spiritual part of ourselves and the divine is the biggest key to transmuting illness in us and in our environment.

In *Be Careful What You Pray For,* Larry Dossey enlightens us with a story that teaches us the importance of being in harmony with ourselves before we can see changes in our environment.

> Richard Wilhelm, the sinologist who translated *The Secret of the Golden Flower: A Chinese Book of Life* and other works, was once in a remote Chinese village that was suffering from an extended drought. Every kind of prayer had been offered to put an end to the drought, but nothing had worked and the people were desperate. The only remaining choice was to send to a remote area for a well-known rainmaker. This fascinated Wilhelm, and he was on hand when the rainmaker, a wizened old man, arrived in a covered cart. He alighted, sniffed the air in disdain, then asked for a cottage on the outskirts of the village. He insisted that he be totally undisturbed and that his food be left outside his door. Nobody heard from him for three days, then the village awoke to a downpour of rain mixed with snow, which was unheard of for that time of year.
>
> Wilhelm, greatly impressed, approached the old man, who was now out of seclusion. "So you can make it rain?" he inquired. Of course he could not, the old man scoffed. "But there was the most persistent drought until you came," Wilhelm objected, "and then—within three days—it rains?" "Oh," responded the man, "that was something quite different. You see, I come from a region where everything is in order, it rains when it should and is fine when that is needed, and the people also are in order and in themselves. But that was not the case with the people here, they were all out of Tao and out of themselves. I was at once infected when I arrived, so I had to be quite alone until I was once more in Tao and then naturally it rained!"
>
> The villagers, the rainmaker saw, were trying to beat the climate into submission when they should have been looking inside.[1]

Among the Salish people who live in the Pacific Northwest, the word *skalatitude* is used to describe what life is like when true kinship with nature exists: "When people and nature are in perfect harmony, then magic and beauty are everywhere."[2]

As you deepen your relationship with the divine in your life, you will find the work of transmutation will take a natural and graceful course. When you connect with nature, you will see that nature is always in harmony with itself.

HOW DO WE SERVE?

One day I was journeying to receive guidance on what I needed to include on returning to a life of harmony with nature. I had a surprising journey, as I received a twist to this aspect of work. First I was shown the image of a German shepherd puppy. I adore German shepherds. The puppy was so loving to me, and I was pouring back love to the puppy. You know how this goes with puppies. I was wondering if the spirits wanted me to get a puppy. But no, they wanted me to get a message.

I was then given the message that the purpose of humans is to nurture. The nature of the human soul is to nurture. When we truly nurture, we don't use our energy. Instead, when we nurture through love and not need, we open the veils between the worlds to work in partnership with the spirits.

Many of us act like children and just take, take, take. We kill animals and plants for ourselves without honoring the life that has been given, and we don't give anything back. As we move more and more toward working with genetically engineered foods, we continue to lose our connection to nature and the true understanding of nurturance.

It is time for us to be adults and nurture through love. If we do not use our nurturing ability, we are blocked. This results in disease and depression. The spirits told me that if people really understood this concept, we wouldn't need antidepressants. I think a lot of people, especially in the helping professions, think they nurture, but they are often living in illusion about the truth of this. Often they are not nurturing from a pure space.

In *Soul Retrieval* I wrote about a journey on which I met an ancient dolphin. He said to me, "The one gift that man has that no other animal has is the ability to pass light through his hands."[3] It is time to let the light inside us, which is a reflection of the light of the divine, pass through us so that we may truly nurture and be of service to the planet.

We really came here to be caretakers of the earth. We are people with a forgotten mission. As we do this we will truly understand the balance of giving and receiving and the spirits really will come through to be in partnership with us. This is our destiny.

HOW ARE YOU NURTURED?

In the previous section I wrote about how we can nurture ourselves emotionally and spiritually by following our destiny to be caretakers of the earth. We must also look at how, as part of nature, we must be nurtured physically. Everything that is alive requires food to grow and thrive. Even the elements provide an example of this. The earth takes up nutrients provided from the sun, water, dead plants, insects, and animals. Air and bodies of water change composition according to what nutrients they are fed. Fire must be fed fuel to keep it burning.

All life eats and changes composition through what it is being fed. However, we don't put sufficient attention into what will support our well-being in this way. In our fast-paced lives we tend to put feeding ourselves at the bottom of our list of priorities. We buy foods that we can cook and eat immediately without attending to the ingredients, the energy that was put into the preparation, the quality of light and nutrition the food holds for us, and the space we create to eat in. We eat as many toxins as nutrients and then wonder why our health fails us. We try to make up for the emptiness in our spiritual, emotional, and physical nurturance by collecting material objects, believing we will receive nurturance in this way.

All life is nurtured and thrives on love. Plants and animals (including humans) that are raised in a loving environment thrive. Although we can sometimes survive in an artificial and nonsupportive environment, the real question is, do we thrive there?

Before a friend of mine died of cancer, she shared with me that she had never appreciated her body as a temple. Before her death she came to this appreciation, but it was too late. The metaphor of the body as a temple is used in different cultures. After all, the body carries our divine spirit as well as being a manifestation of the divine. It is important to honor the body and support it in whatever ways we can.

○ EXERCISES

Here are some questions to meditate on and/or journal on to start looking at how you nurture others and how you nurture yourself.

How do you nurture yourself, others, and the earth?

Do you see yourself as a caretaker of the earth? If your answer to this question is no, more work is necessary. What do the words "caretaker of the earth" mean to you? What metaphors can you use to get the true meaning of this? What is something you can begin to do now to move your creative energy to a place of service and caretaking?

Do you nurture more from a place of need or through true, pure love? Can you think of an example of a time when you gave of yourself from a pure and unconditional place? How did you feel afterward?

What shifts can you make in your work and life to bring you to a true place of really nurturing others and yourself?

How do you feed yourself? Notice whether the food you eat provides you with the nutrients to fill every one of your cells with light, energy, power, and life. When you eat, ask yourself this question: Are you being nurtured from this food?

Do you put time and care into shopping for foods that will nurture you? Do you put time and love into food preparation? Do you create a peaceful environment to eat in? Do you relax during your meal? If your answer to any of these questions is no, please list priorities that you feel are more important. Are these really more important than your health and well-being?

There are times when we cannot control what we put into our bodies, as so much of our food is affected by toxins in the soil and environment. This is where we need to rely on our transmutation abilities. A ceremony for working with food is given in Part VI, "Ceremonies for Transmutation."

Working with Cycles and Rhythms in Nature

One of the premises in *Medicine for the Earth* is that we are caught up in the illusions we have created; we are dreaming the wrong dream. We moved from living a life fully connected to and celebrating the forces of nature to living in a scientific, technological society ruled by the rational mind. Being ruled only by the rational mind has limited our vision, so there is not much breath or spiritual expansion to our lives. This is one reason why working with metaphor is so healing for us—it returns breath and spiritual expansion to how we experience the world by expressing thoughts and emotions that "true" stories can't express. We have made ourselves smaller spiritually in order to survive in our society. We have learned not to take up space. This is a cause of physical illness and much of the depression and anxiety we experience today. We do not know how to move with or work with the creative fire that is burning inside us.

One cure for depression and anxiety is to expand. We must reach out with our energy. To do this, we must ignite all of our senses. We live in a culture obsessed with visual information and stimulation. But sight is not our most evolved sense. We must once again feel, hear, smell, and taste life around us. This will aid in expanding our energy and let us experience the natural world of which we are a part.

Nature can teach us how to move aside the veils of illusion and get back to a life filled with truth. In order to do this, we must connect with the monthly cycles of the moon and seasonal changes of the earth. As we watch how the moon and sun move across the sky and how these movements change with the changing times of year, we become part of the web of all life again. As we learn to open all our senses, we can forecast the coming seasonal changes without needing a calendar. As we experience the ebb and flow of nature, we will learn that we are never blocked creatively, but are part of a natural process. As we experience fully what happens in our environment during seasonal changes, we remember that a major lesson in life is that all life is change. We have created rigid routines that put stress on us and block our connection with nature. We need to learn how to flow with the energy instead of suffer from the energy. As we celebrate the changes in the season, we remember that change is to be welcomed and not feared. One might ask if ancient celebrations of the cycles of the moon, the sun, and other forces in the natural world were really primitive rituals worshiping false gods. I don't believe so. Celebrating seasonal changes is one way we honor and harmonize with the earth's cycles that governs us. Honoring the cycles of our external world enables us to re-create this harmony within ourselves and, by extension, within our communities. And as we see the beauty in all things, the veils of illusion begin to lift and we can once again discover the secrets of the magic of life. In this way we harmonize with ourselves, the earth, and the absolute joy of creation.

THE MOON

The great circular moon continually orbits the earth, sometimes apparent and sometimes invisible to our eye. It can take on a silvery hue or it can look golden. It shines down on us as a giant orb sitting in the night sky. Sometimes we can see a glimpse of it in the daytime. It takes on different shapes at different phases of the month. At times it completely disappears and then reappears to our wonderment as a tiny sliver against its background of night. The moon really has no color of its own; the colorful shine comes from the sun's reflection upon it. The full moon rises and sets high in the sky in winter and low in the sky during the summer. The moon's magnetic energy rules the tides, the growth of plants, and the cycles of life.

For thousands of years people all over the world lived in accordance with the moon's cycles. We can still remember stories of how our ancestors planted to the moon's cycles, and many tales of how the moon's phase affects our activities, such as the best phase to cut hair in or how rubbing a wart with a slice of potato and planting the potato during the full moon will cause the wart to disappear. The *Farmer's Almanac* is full of these tales.

Songs, poems, and ceremonies have been created since the beginning of time to honor the moon. Some cultures called the moon Grandmother Moon, some Grandfather Moon. Think of all the songs and stories in modern times written to the man in the moon. For some the moon will take on a female energy; for others it is male. But the moon is all these energies. It is both male and female, and we project certain qualities onto the moon depending on what we need at the time.

As we are mostly water, the moon's magnetic energy will have a different effect on our moods and energy with each phase. The energy of the waning moon will affect us differently than when it is at its fullest. The magnetic energy at times draws us deep inside ourselves and at other times draws us out more into the world. To flow with the river of life rather than against it, we need to discover during what phases we are more introverted and what phases support our creative social expression in the world.

○ EXERCISES

It is important not to turn to someone else's interpretation of how you should feel during various phases of the moon. This is for you to discover. How does your own rhythm dance to the cycles of the moon? Here are some ways to discover this.

The best way to discover the effect that the moon has on you is to be observant and record your moods and energy levels with each phase. Notice differences when the moon is waning and when the moon is waxing. After you have been doing this for a number of months, read back over your journal to observe patterns. Keep your journaling very simple. Just use a few words that will help you remember your moods and energy levels. You want to note whether you were feeling reclusive and withdrawn or extroverted and social. Note whether you needed more sleep and had very little energy or if your energy level was high and you felt motivated to be creative. Note whether you felt happy and peaceful or grumpy and depressed. Note your quality of sleep at different phases, including whether it was fitful or deep. Notice if the quality of your dreams changes at different phases. Don't write about the day's events. Just use key words that will help you decipher rhythms.

After you have established these patterns, it is time to look at how you need to change your life to harmonize with the moon's cycles. Look at changes you can make in your routine that will nurture your connection with your own lunar cycle. Examples would include creating alone time when the magnetic energy is pulling you inside yourself, scheduling social events when the energy is supporting you being extroverted, visioning when your creative energy is drawn inward, and taking action and putting projects into physical motion when you are being drawn out of yourself. Think of a plant that draws in nurturance, supporting growth under the dark, rich earth before bursting forth into the world. There are times when the seeds need to be nourished before growth can happen. There are times when the roots need to be nourished for a healthy plant to grow.

Using automatic writing, write a story about the connection of your cycles to the moon's phases.

Use methods from previous chapters to get into a very relaxed meditative state. Visualize the moon shining above you in the night sky. Speak to the moon, directing questions to the moon itself about how you can harmonize with its cycles.

Meditate on the following questions:

How am I nurtured by the moon's light?

How is my growth best supported by the moon's light?

Using the principle of "As above, so below; as within, so without," how can I nurture the moon's light inside of me?

THE SUN

People all over the world have celebrated and worshiped the power of the sun. Without sunlight to nurture us, there would be no life. The Egyptians sang homage to the sun god, Ra, whose manifestations made the world bright and light. The Sami people of northern Europe believed in the healing power of the sun, and the shamans invoked this power in their healings; the same is true for many other cultures. Sun is life, and this life force can be called upon for healing. In modern cultures people flock to beaches in summer in a form of worship. Today, scientists are finding that being in the sun just ten minutes a day can reduce cancer. It is also being found that children who spend time in the sun have better concentration skills. Unfortunately, today the sun can also cause cancer due to reduced ozone levels.

The sun was worshiped for the light it shared on all levels. Manly Hall says the sun reflected the light of the invisible spiritual sun—the true source of light.[1]

Caroline Casey adds to the alchemical view of working with the sun:

In alchemy, the Great Work is called the Operation of the Sun, which is the full cultivation of the human personality as a translucent vessel through which life can shine. The living gold of which the alchemists spoke is manifest in the radiant energy of the Sun. The Sun is our guiding light, reminding us that we are incarnations of all the gods. All the planets, gods, and forces of our psyche reflect the light of the Sun.[2]

Recent scientific evidence is showing that one reason for the fall of Egypt, Babylon, and Rome leading to the dark ages was due to collisions with comets or fragments of comets where the explosive energy caused dust and smoke dimming the sun, driving down temperatures, and causing famine.

In *Catastrophe: A Quest for the Origins of the Modern World*, British historian David Keys describes a time when the sun became dark for two years in A.D. 535, affecting all of life from California to Ireland to Siberia, decimating life in Italy, China, and the Middle East.

Research has shown that environmental disasters such as this occurred around 3200 B.C., 2300 B.C., 1628 B.C., and 1159 B.C. Civilization as we know it was wiped out during these times.[3]

We are dependent on the sun to live. Without the sun there are no food sources. As animals we need to eat. The sun not only provides us with food, but also the cycles of the sun govern our seasons. Through observation, people have been able to prepare for the changes that occur during different seasons. By watching the migration of certain birds, they could tell the beginning of a change in season. When nature provides a lot of fruit and berries, it can indicate a hard, long winter ahead.

We are no longer good observers of the wildlife and plant life around us, which signals the changes in our seasons. We rely on calendars and predictions from news reports of what kind of season we will have. We have cut ourselves off from a rich connection, which would virtually feed our souls, igniting our natural instincts, putting us in touch with our own natural intuition.

When I used to work as a psychotherapist, I was in awe of how many clients would report in autumn that they felt like they were dying. I used to ask if they had looked outside to see what was happening in nature. In our lives, we have many little deaths; these deaths are necessary for our continued growth and evolution. We are always dying so we can live. All life has cycles of death so that life might continue. We cannot stop these little deaths or changes in nature from happening without consequences. Regeneration is a part of life. As we don't always know what little deaths are part of our destiny, we must put our trust and faith in our spirit and the power of the universe to help us release that which no longer serves us. Our only role during this time is to be like the tree who remembers its true nature and gracefully lets go of its leaves to return to the earth.

In winter, what has died feeds the earth. The snow and cold actually allow a furnace to burn inside the earth, which gives the seeds the ability to burst forth in the spring.

The spring is when the last frost of winter leaves, and we see the new life beginning to form. This reminds us that with all death and change, new beginnings can be birthed. We think of planting seeds that will be fed by the warmth of the earth and the light of the sun, producing the vegetables, fruits, and flowers that provide us with nourishment on all levels. We think of animals mating, so the young will have the time to learn to thrive before the cold returns.

In summer, we enjoy the fruits of all our labors. Life is at its fullest. It is the time to collect the nourishment the earth offers us and the power of the light of the sun to get us through the dark times ahead.

Wildlife also changes its behavior with the movement of the sun and seasons. The wind changes with each season, as does the temperature, the humidity, the scent in the air. The colors of the sky as well as the positions of the sun and moon change, too. As our environment and the light of the sun changes, so do our moods and energy levels.

If we are living in accordance with the laws of nature, we find ourselves needing to live, sleep, and eat differently during different seasons. To be in the current of the river of life, we cannot keep to the same routine 365 days a year, but many of us try. This is against the laws of nature.

○ EXERCISES

Observation is the key to learning how the cycles of the sun affect us and the rest of life. If you live in a city, you might need to get out to a natural environment to study the changes in the seasons.

Take note of what wildlife is more active in your area at different times of the year. Watch animal behavior as the seasons change. Notice what birds migrate to your area at different times. Learn how to tell the changing seasons by what the plant life is doing. Experience the quality changes in the air and learn the smells and tastes of each arriving season. Touch the earth, noticing how the ground feels with each changing season. Follow the wind, rain, and snow patterns for each season. Take note of the temperature changes. Use the elements you see, feel, smell, hear, and taste to inform you of the change in seasons.

As you become more proficient in your observation skills, you will be able to not just predict a new season coming but also tell what kind of a season it will be—a long or short fall, a mild or harsh winter, a wet or dry spring, a moderate or intense summer. There are numerous benefits to doing this. You will once again be part of nature. This will bring a beauty, depth, richness, and connection back into your life, as you notice changes in the life around you.

Take note of your nature during the seasons. How do your energy levels and sleep needs change? What types of foods are you drawn to at different times of the year? When do you want to be introspective and when do you want to be more social? Do you have any hibernation needs for regeneration? When do you want to plant seeds of creative projects? When do you need to gestate the seeds you plant? When do you find yourself birthing the seeds you have planted?

What changes do you need to make in your life and activities to support and nourish the changes of the seasons in you? How can you once again attune to the forces of nature that change your lifestyle from a place of disharmony to harmony?

The next time you attempt a creative project, use what you have learned from watching the seasons. Look at what you need to do to prepare and nourish the ground before you plant your creative seeds. Once you have planted the seeds, let the germination happen in its own time—don't push the river. So much unseen life is growing during the dark, inactive times. Weed out the weak growth from the strong growth as the creative force begins to surface. Follow the energy of the creative fire as it burns bright in the summer of your project. Celebrate and reward yourself as you watch the fruits of your labor burst forth in a natural way.

Nature is simply spectacular; the beauty and complexity of life stops the mind. Take a walk, simply admiring and appreciating the natural world. Get out and simply enjoy and soak in the beauty of nature around you. As you move into a state of deep appreciation for the beauty you are seeing, shine your own light back to the life around you, stepping into your role as caretaker of the earth.

You will notice as you begin to harmonize with the cycles of the moon and sun that nature brings you to an understanding about ebb and flow. One must take time to retreat to be nourished and rejuvenate before creativity can flow again. Make sure you are nurturing yourself and feeding your own light. Think about what this means to you and how you can best nurture your own "shine." Think of yourself as a growing plant. A plant puts forth beautiful blooms when it has the energy to do so. The more it is fed, the less energy it needs for growth. If at any point your growth requires too much effort, try to find the needed nourishment. If a plant does not rest and receive nourishment after blooming, the next bloom will be small or withered. This is your responsibility. The river of life will take you to many places, but you must feed yourself along the way. Don't expect to be on, creative, and productive all the time. This is not natural and doesn't support healthy growth.

Remember the nature of the human soul is to nurture the earth. You must learn how your own light needs to be nourished and supported, so you can be a caretaker of the earth.

12

Working with the Elements

Earth, air, water, fire—they are in us as well as all around us. Our bodies are the earth for our spirit. Our blood is the waterway that carries nutrients to our cells. Fire burns deep inside of us keeping the spark of life alive, reflecting the deep fire that burns inside the earth. The air we breathe from outside to inside of us is essential for life to continue. We can live without food or water for days, but we can survive without air for only minutes at a time.

The earth is the body that provides our foundation to walk and live on, as well as the plant life we need to sustain our bodies. The plants are fed rich nutrients through their roots, which they then can transfer to us. The fire inside the earth keeps her life force burning. The bright power of the fiery sun gives power to the plants that is also passed on to us. We collect the power of the sun that stimulates life, light, and growth on many levels. We all know what happens to us when we don't see the sun for days. Some people go into depressed states emotionally and physically when the power of light, which feeds our bodies, minds, and souls, is not present.

Water is life. Where there is no water, there is no life. Every life form on this planet must have water to survive. Water brings nutrients to our cells as well as cleanses us of toxins. When I was considering my first pilgrimage to Egypt, I journeyed to my spiritual teacher,

Isis, to ask her advice. She was thrilled that I was finally willing to take the physical journey to visit her home. She left me with an intriguing message: "The power of a place is the water that runs through it." I knew she was referring to the Nile river, her home. But this message left me pondering the issue of water creating power in a place. We know the obvious power the ocean and rivers bring to places, as people flock to locations where they can experience these mighty forces. But even in desert areas, power is brought to the land through the deep channels of water that run through it.

Living in Santa Fe, I experience a very deep and silent power in the land. The water also runs deep and silent through the earth here. I realized one could begin to identify certain qualities of power by looking at the water sources that feed and run through the land.

Air is not only required so we can breathe, but it is also a carrier of life forms from place to place. Air movement manifesting as breezes to strong winds transport pollens and seeds, creating plant life whose beauty and nutrients feed us. Nutrients are carried through the air, which feed the earth and water, as well as the fire deep in the earth. Tribal people believed the wind was the carrier of messages to life forms across the land. The wind signals changes in weather as well as seasons. The wind brings relief from pollution.

The interconnectedness of all things in nature is truly wondrous. And to continue with one of the underlying themes in this book—as above, so below; as within, so without—we can examine and appreciate how the elements are with us on many levels. We also learn that the elements are living beings and need to be treated as such.

If we were to imagine ourselves as a visitor to the earth and we observed the behavior of humans, some questions that might arise would be:

Why do humans dump chemicals and toxins onto the earth, which provides nutrition, toxifying food?
Why do humans dump toxins and poisons in the water, which

goes into growing food, being absorbed by every cell in the body?

How can the water of life cleanse the cells and organs of the body when the water is toxic itself?

Why do humans pump pollutants into the air, which they then breathe? Why do humans pollute the air, which affects the sun, the giver of life?

Why do humans poison the elements, which are living beings?

I wonder how you as a tourist from another galaxy would perceive the behavior of these humans.

Although the elements are living beings they are also neutral energy. When an earthquake occurs, the earth is not considering the impact on humans, fires don't burn down houses as a personal issue, floods don't have an agenda, the wind just blows without thinking about effects. The forces of nature are always in harmony and at the same time neutral.

I know in my own life I have had extreme lessons and experiences about the power and neutrality of the elements. In the early 1970s, I was overcome by the power of the ocean and had a near-death experience through drowning. In the late 1970s, I was a forest fire fighter for a summer and learned about the power of fire. In the early 1980s, I was almost flattened and killed by an eight-ton boulder flying down Mt. Shasta while I was climbing. And later on in the 1980s, I was in a plane that lost control on landing in the wind currents. On all these occasions, I experienced how the elements simply live and move through our world as well as the force behind them.

There's a lot we can learn from studying the elements. As we observe the elements around us, it might help us understand how they move through us. As we comprehend how essential the elements are to our health, we will begin to honor all they bring to us and perhaps we will become better caretakers of the earth. As we learn that the elements are living beings, we will understand how to care for them. In the meantime, we will need to learn how to transmute the toxins and poisons polluting all the elements outside and inside us.

○ Exercises

First, begin by observing the elements around you. Explore the earth you live on, get to know your water sources, look at how the water that runs through the land affects the quality of the power of the land, take in the air around you, absorb the power of the sun representing the element of fire. Experience how they are alive.

Give these sources of life a small gift of thanks for your life. In North America, pure tobacco or cornmeal were given as offerings. Some cultures give rice, others offer lavender, and still others make gifts of food, especially sweets. Think about what you would like to give from your heart that has meaning to you. Honoring the elements in this way will establish a relationship with this part of the web of life.

A powerful way of learning about the elements is to merge with each one individually. To do this you must enter a deep meditative state—for you want to lose yourself and become one with the element you are merging with. This is an allowing process; you cannot do it with your mind, you must sink into the experience.

As water, you might become a drop of rain, or a tear running down a face, or you might become the ocean itself, or a drop from a river going down a waterfall, or you might become fine mist bringing life to plants, or a dew drop on a leaf, or a snowflake.

As air, you might become the mighty wind, or you might be the quiet stillness of the air on a perfect summer day, or you might be a gentle breeze moving through the grass or trees, or the great gusts surfing through the landscape.

As earth, you might be a grain of sand that drifts through eternity, or a plot of earth being fed nutrients from the other elements. You might become the earth of a desert, a tropical island, or a rain forest.

As fire, you might become a raging fire, or the small bright flame of a birthday candle, or a flame of a candle burning at a romantic dinner, or the fire in a volcano, or the fire of a beautiful sunrise or sunset.

Do this exercise over time. Don't attempt to merge with all the elements in one day. You will not have the time to process the material and receive the learning you need. You might choose to work with one element for a month or in one particular season.

I have been experimenting with the transmutation of toxins in water. In workshops I use the exercise of merging with water as preparation for our ceremony (see Epilogue). The reports I have received are that people find this work to change their relationship with water as the merging left them with the ineffable feeling that water is a living being. I have received love/hate mail around this as one can no longer wash dishes, flush toilets, or watch ocean waves without the conscious realization that they are interacting with a living being. This is actually the effect you are trying to achieve.

In merging with the elements, we also learn that it is movement that keeps the elements healthy. For example, as we pollute water, the movement of the molecules is decreased, which decreases its life force, health, and purity. Pollution creates energy that becomes stuck; vital energy is always moving.

There is great teaching that can come from taking a walk in nature and opening yourself up to receive a message from the earth you walk or sit on, the air around you—what message does the still air, a breeze, or wind bring to you, a message from a small or large body of water you can sit with, or a fire you can meditate on through watching the flame of a candle or the flames burning at a campfire?

You can receive messages from nature, but once again you must quiet your rational mind to do so. You must get into a quiet space and then notice as you ask each element for a message if you get a visual image, an auditory message, a feeling in your body, a particular smell, or taste.

This is a classic method that comes from the practice of shamanism, in which the shaman opens his or her invisible senses to receive deep wisdom from the natural world.

As you walk in nature, notice if a song comes to you. Often I find myself singing a song that arises from my heart, asking for blessings from an element I am appreciating. Or you can give yourself permission to spontaneously hum, allowing the spirit of the earth to sing through you. I feel a tremendous amount of power in my body after a walk when I do this. As children, we sang to nature. Allow your childlike innocence to return to help you with this.

As you work with the elements individually, you will notice that as you walk outside, you are naturally aware of all the elements around you without having to concentrate on them:

What element or elements are you attracted to working with?
   What qualities do you like about the element?
What element or elements are you afraid of? What brings up fear for you?
What element or elements do you feel unfamiliar with?

Work with an element you have too much of. For example, if you are anxious, do you have too much fire? How can you temper it or channel this fire energy creatively?

What element do you think you might be missing?

What element would be balancing for you to call into your life?

Think about how the elements live in your own body. How do you nourish and take care of your body—earth? How pure is the water bringing nutrients to you? How is the fire of life burning inside of you—does it need to be calmed or fed? How is the air moving through you—does your breath bring oxygen to all your cells?

These suggestions might stimulate your imagination to come up with ways to experience the elements on your own. The key is to remember our interconnectedness with the forces of life.

Here is a meditation you can use to connect you with the elements in your life:

> Imagine yourself being in a meadow filled with your favorite flowers.
> You are one of these flowers.
> You feel yourself being nurtured by the gentle breezes.
> You feel yourself being nurtured by the sun above.
> You receive deeply the nurturance of the soil below you.
> You receive joyfully the nurturance from the rain upon you.
> Receive the nurturance of these life-giving elements, and give back to them with your eternal light.

> Repeat this exercise when you need to restore and regenerate.

13

A Shift of Perception

When we were children, we knew that there was a spirit that lived in all things. We spoke to invisible beings, trees, the sky, the moon, the birds, our animals, etc. People all over the world have been doing this for thousands of years. In our socialization process, we were taught how to live and behave in modern society. The doors between the worlds closed for most of us as we were told to stop talking to our imaginary friends. The invisible worlds were invalidated for us. This action has changed the course in human history, as the spiritual worlds became less accessible to us, so did the magic of life.

Once you harmonize and begin to work with becoming more observant in the natural world, the veil between the rational and invisible worlds begins to open. You will find that you will have a different connection with plants, trees, animals, insects, and rocks. You will begin to receive messages from these living beings that can take the form of visions, feelings, telepathic messages, smells, and tastes. We must once again reignite our invisible senses to be open to the wisdom of the life forms we share this planet with. In *Soul Retrieval,* I shared a journey of a Siberian shaman who kept instructing people she met along the way to "close your thick ears and open your thin ears." This is a metaphor of what needs to happen to be in touch with the senses that open us up to a reality we have forgotten.

People who have lived and still live in indigenous cultures have always talked to the spirit of plants, trees, animals, rocks, the elements, and all living beings. Information on what plants would cure certain illnesses came from the plant itself. The information of where people could find food sources came from the animals and the reading of omens given by nature. Living beings have a wealth of information to share with us humans, but we cannot communicate with these beings in an ordinary state of consciousness.

George Washington Carver and Luther Burbank are examples of respected botanists who made great contributions to their field. George Washington Carver said that he gained his knowledge about cultivating plants from walking through the forests and talking to them. Luther Burbank conducted many successful plant-breeding experiments. He introduced more than 800 new varieties of plants. Burbank was also known to speak with the spirits of the plants he worked with.[1]

Today, we rely on many plants from the rain forests of South America to cure a variety of diseases. The shamans in these areas identified what plants would cure what illness by observing their shape as well as speaking with them while in an altered state of consciousness.

Besides talking to the spirit in the life forms we can actually see, there are other types of nature spirits that people around the world have communicated with. Some traditions work with devas and fairies, magical beings which inhabit the land where we live. By calling in and working in partnership with these beings, one can begin to manifest changes in the land. Findhorn, in Scotland, is a spiritual community, which began in 1962. It was world renowned for what we would consider having miraculous gardens. The plants and vegetables created awe not only by their beauty and their impossible size but also by how they were grown in adverse conditions. For years people flocked to Findhorn from all over the world to be dazzled with the miracle of life. Perelandra, started in Virginia by Michaelle Small Wright, is another example of a miraculous garden grown by forming a creative partnership with the nature spirits. Large healthy plants are grown with no chemicals or pesticides. Just imagine the energy you could receive by eating plants grown in such a harmonious and magical fashion.

In Iceland, the government and construction crews work with the "hidden folk"—elves, dwarves, and fairies. Maps are drawn indicating where they live, and new construction must take into account the "little people's" homes. Construction companies have found that if they negotiate their building plans with the "little people" before bringing in construction equipment, money is saved. Otherwise everything goes wrong—machines break or workers become ill—doubling or tripling building costs.

It is time to return to a lifestyle where we form a creative partnership with the nature spirits. First, there must be the desire on our part. Then we must focus our intention and concentration on calling on the nature spirits. We must be able to imagine that such a partnership is possible. And if we come from a place of love, the nature spirits will respond to us. As we realize that we are part of the trees, the plants, the insects, the birds, the animals, the rocks, the water, the fire, the air, the earth, the sun, the moon, the clouds, and the stars, we create the principle of union and harmony that completes the formula for transmutation. In this way, we will begin to see that the pollution and toxins that we have created from a place of disharmony and separation naturally begin to heal on their own.

Every life form on this planet has an intelligence. Just observe how different life forms live, collect food and nutrition, and survive in adverse conditions, and you will know inside yourself the truth that all life is intelligent. Not only do human beings and nature transmute substances, but other life forms also do, an example being bees, who at some point in making honey transmute some of it into royal jelly. The only thing that separates us from the rest of life is that our destiny is to caretake the earth so that all life might thrive.

As we continue on a path of disharmony, we find that the elements are acting in an extreme and violent fashion. We must question whether our own disharmony and violence is being mirrored back to us by nature. Earthquakes are happening with more frequency, fires are raging through the earth, hurricanes and tornadoes shake up life, and then we have extremes with floods and drought. As the weather has become more extreme and violent, people are starting to search out and learn from indigenous people who have long worked with the weather spirits. In 1998, five months of El Niño brought a drought to the Amazon region near the Brazilian border of Venezuela. Fires began to rage, killing huge populations of animals and destroying millions of acres of land. Technology could offer no help in this situation. The Brazilian shamans came to the rescue. They summoned the spirits, they danced and sang and performed rituals. The rains came and the fires went out.

The Hopi Indians of the southwestern United States are known for their ability to work with the weather. They have also been called into areas of extreme drought. The shamans of China called for rain by performing special dances. It's important to note that the laws of the universe do not support those who use spiritual methods to manipulate the environment. The key here is not manipulation but partnership. The key is returning to a place of harmony, so the weather that will support life can return. Some suggestions for working with the weather spirits will be given in Part VI.

You can use many of the exercises that I have presented in the different sections of this chapter to work with the material in this section. You want to observe the forces of nature where you live, to receive messages from them by quieting your mind and opening up a line of communication where you will receive wisdom in invisible ways.

You might wish to begin by working with a favorite plant that is growing in your garden or in a park you like to visit. Sit with this plant and let yourself drift into a state where you can speak to the plant. You don't want to speak out loud. This is a process that requires you to be in a quiet state. You can do this same process with the rocks, insects, birds, and animals that are around you. Naturally, you might not get an insect, bird, or animal to sit still for you. But you can communicate with them as they move through your field of vision. In this way, you can turn to nature itself for direct revelation on how to once again live in harmony and be a caretaker for the earth.

Using the formula for transmutation of intention, love, harmony, union, focus, concentration, and imagination, call in the nature spirits to the place where you live. Observe any differences in yourself and the place where you live as you do this.

THE POWER OF PLACE

People around the world have always recognized that the place where one lives has a spirit. The spirit of this place was honored and called on in ceremonies for healing as well as for celebration at different times of the year. Once again, to live in harmony, the spirit of all things must be recognized on all levels.

As we have left our own spiritual traditions, we lost a valuable resource—the power of place. Every piece of land is inhabited not only by nature spirits but also by its own inherent spirit. As the earth is alive where we live and work, these places have a spirit, too. And this spirit can be called on to create a harmonious partnership as well as to offer power and support.

Today, when groups gather to perform rituals and ceremonies, the spirit of the place is often not honored. We assume that we can walk on to any piece of land and do our work. While this is probably true, let's not forget what we have been taught about being polite. Use common courtesy before doing spiritual work at a site—introduce yourself to the spirit of the land and state your intention. You will find that more power is available to you for the work you plan to do.

If you can introduce yourself to the spirit of the place where you live and work, you will also find that a connection and an alignment is created to a power source that can lend support and wisdom in your life. This is especially important if you live in a city where its spirit is not obvious to you, as it is covered up by cement and build-ings. Before traveling, journey or meditate to meet the spirit of the city or country you are visiting. This will create a relationship that will give you a richer and deeper experience in your travels. Connecting with the spirit of place continues the work of creating union, a key element in our work with transmutation, as once again we honor all life.

○ EXERCISES

Walk around the neighborhood where you live. Notice if there is a spot of land that seems to call to you. Have a seat and quiet your mind. Use your breath to get the energy moving through your body, and open your heart. From your heart, introduce yourself to the spirit of the place and let the spirit know you would like to connect with it. Tell the spirit you honor it, and thank the spirit for providing such a wonderful place to live. Ask the spirit of this place if there is a small gift of thanks that you could leave that would honor it.

Open up your invisible senses and notice if you get any kind of acknowledgment from the spirit here. As you build a relationship with the spirit here, this place will become a power spot for you—a place you can return to for regeneration, peace of mind, and healing. You might also notice your life flows more easily as you establish a connection with the life force of where you live.

You can repeat this same procedure to connect with the power of place of where you work.

If you live in a city, you might wish at some point to establish connection with a place in a park or the countryside that can serve as a place of power, healing, and regeneration for you.

EXPERIENCING HEAVEN ON EARTH

My dream, my desire, my intent in this lifetime is to experience heaven on earth. When I teach my workshops on shamanism, one of the first ceremonies we perform in the group is to call down the helping spirits, who will teach us, support us, and lend us help for ourselves and the entire group. I believe it is important to state our intention to the spirits. Otherwise, it is like calling someone up on the telephone and not saying anything. Eventually, the person you called will hang up the phone on you. As I use my rattle to call down the spirits, I always state a silent intention that I wish for the group to experience heaven on earth.

As I was journeying on writing this chapter I received a powerful message. I was told it's important to realize that there is no separation between heaven and earth. An illusion creates this perceived separation. Once again I was told that we have closed the veils between the worlds with our egos and minds.

As I continued to work with this issue I was shown I must see the beauty in everything throughout the day. I was told by my helping spirits that when I could accomplish this, my perception would shift.

In Chapter 8, I focused on creating a different reality through the use of imagination. The next step for deepening this process is understanding that when your perception shifts, your reality changes.

The following exercise was given to me in my journey to remedy the perceived separation between heaven and earth:

See the beauty in everything, every minute of the day. The first step to seeing the beauty in all things is to be in a state of deep appreciation.

This practice will open the veils between the worlds. It is not easy to accomplish this task. Have patience with yourself. Everyday, keep opening your perception to see the beauty in everyone and all things around you. Everyday, you will be able to concentrate on this a little more and a little more. As you can imagine, soon you will view life in a whole different way, changing your reality.

To heal the earth through transmutation, you must connect with the elements, the plants, the animals, and all forces of nature. You must reestablish your connection with the web of life, seeing that you are not separate from the rest of life, and you must see the beauty in all things. By shifting your perception, you will change your reality.

Parts of formula for transmutation used here:

Intention: You must set a strong intention to return to living in accordance with the laws of nature, remembering you are part of the web of life and are ruled by, and a part of, the cycles of nature. You must set an intention to open the lines of communication with the spirit that lives in all things.

Love: As you open up to the wisdom of the trees, the plants, the animals, the insects, the sun, the moon, the stars, and the elements, you learn that all life thrives on love, and love is a key to creating harmony.

Harmony: If you return harmony to yourself by aligning yourself with the river of life, the river of life will bring harmony back to you and the planet.

Union: When you remember your connection to the web of life and the spirit that lives in all things, you are once again in union with yourself, the rest of life, and the divine.

Focus: You must focus on your intention to open the lines of communication with the spirits of nature.

Concentration: You must concentrate on intentionally changing your way of life to once again return to harmony with yourself and the natural world.

Imagination: You must be able to imagine the spirits and forces of nature that live around you, the forces of nature that live in you, and a world in harmony and balance again. You must be able to use your imagination to see the beauty in all things.

Your attention turns to the bowls of polluted water that sit in the center of your circle. The vibration of love coming through you joins with the vibration of this water. The light of the divine infuses the water. Harmony within; harmony without. This polluted water transmutes to holy water.

Imagine.

V

Transmutation

Imagine inviting a small group of your community to ga[...]
form a ceremony of transmutation. You have cleared out a ro[...]
house. Everyone brings flowers and special objects that remin[...]
their connection with the divine. Together you create sacred spa[...]
room.

You have spent days preparing for the work that is about to[...]
You have paid special attention to your diet, activities, and thoug[...]
place you into a sacred space where you have focused your attentio[...]
your relationship to the divine aspects in you and around you.

You invoke the spirit of love and light. You call forth the divine. Y[...]
begin letting the energy of the space you are in sing through you. Ton[...]
and chants coming from the group create a harmony inside each of you[...]
as well as set up a vibration that melts away any veils between the worlds.

14

Embodying the Divine

The high road, as distinguished from the low road, is the
way of the alchemist, whose heart is in the shining glory all
the day and all the way that his pilgrim feet walk the dusty
ways of man—transmuting, transmuting, and transmuting
that dust into purest radiance.

— ST. GERMAIN

There are different ways that the divine can be invoked for miracles to take place. One way is through direct divine intervention. This is where the compassion of the divine manifests to intervene on your behalf for healing. This is what occurs when one is healed through embarking on a spiritual pilgrimage to healing sites. Thousands of pilgrims who have journeyed to such places recount miraculous healings. Reports of the crippled throwing down crutches, the blind having sight returned, cancerous tumors disappearing, and other forms of pain and suffering being alleviated have inspired and mystified us. We have people relating visions of an array of spiritual figures and saints such as Jesus, Mary, Sai Baba, Buddha, Shiva, Kuan Yin, or Isis coming to them and bringing healing to the body and soul.

In many of these cases healing has been prayed for. But sometimes the healing comes spontaneously, without a conscious request. We cannot perform an autopsy on the miracle of divine intervention.

This belongs to the great mysteries of life. Whether this type of miracle is prayed for or whether it just comes, all who experience this type of healing have been blessed by the compassionate power of the divine.

As this form of healing does transmute toxins, pain, and suffering, I mention it here. But it is not the focus of this part, as I am preparing you to step into the role of transmuter. Jesus performed many miracles, but he tried to teach us that we could, too. One way to transmute energy is to call forth the power of the divine to work through you. You must become an empty vessel to work in this way. The spiritual practices given in the previous parts of this book have provided a means to prepare you for this powerful work. If you have committed deeply and with full intention and focus to the spiritual practices I have suggested, you now hold the consciousness and awareness needed to work in the way the creator intended.

The key now is to add the principle of embodying the divine to what you have learned about being in union with the divine. By becoming the creator, the absolute, you have been working with, you embody this energy. There is a different quality to the notion of "embodying" than to the concept of "union." Union is formless. Embodying implies that you are now containing this formless energy and bringing it through for the purpose of transmutation.

There are a couple of ways to embody the divine. One way is to call down the power of the creator, god, goddess, or other spiritual energies that you have been working with to merge with you and work through you. Using the principle of "As above, so below; as within, so without," you can call forth that same divinity that resides in you. In the pictographs on the walls of the temples in Egypt one often sees depicted the earthly form of the god or goddess next to the deity's heavenly form. For example, at Edfu, in the temple for the god Horus, the holy child, one constantly sees depicted the earthly form of Horus as well as his heavenly form. I interpret this to mean that we all have our earthly or human form. But inside of us also resides the heavenly or divine aspect. This heavenly or divine aspect of ourselves can be called forth to provide the love, light, and healing energies needed for transmutation to occur. We will explore how to identify this heavenly aspect of ourselves later on in this chapter.

To embody the divine, we must have a body, a container that can handle the vibration needed to perform such powerful healing work. I must remind you again that it is important to incorporate physical practices such as yoga, tai chi, chi gong, and so on, which are aimed at creating a strong body that can contain such powerful spiritual energies. You don't want to blow yourself out, as can happen to an electric appliance when it is plugged into a socket that has a greater voltage than it has been adapted for. Performing this kind of spiritual work requires a key ingredient—power. The Hindus call this *shakti.* The Hindu path of tantra is devoted to transmutation, and the development of shakti is part of this ancient spiritual practice. The Hindus also use the word *prana,* while in China this power is called *chi.*

In October 1999 I returned to Egypt. My first trip to Egypt, in 1998, precipitated the beginning of this book. My second trip came just before I was to finish this chapter. I was once again leading a spiritual pilgrimage, and I requested permission to have my group spend the night in the Great Pyramid on Halloween. Permission was granted. As I knew that this was an extraordinary gift for the group, I did a lot of journeying in preparation.

In my journeys I received information on the nature of the Great Pyramid. There are many theories about the mysteries of the Great Pyramid. I do not pretend to have authority or the final word on what this great structure was and is about. The ancient Egyptians were a civilization unto themselves, one that we may never comprehend. But I was shown what was important for me and my group to work with in the evening ceremony. In my understanding, the Great Pyramid was used for initiation. There are three chambers in the

Great Pyramid. For the purposes of our work, the Lower Chamber was to be seen as the womb, the great void from which we came, the place of unlimited possibilities. As we chose to enter this world with the remembrance of our soul's purpose intact, we began in the womb. This is the beginning. As we were nurtured and formed and shaped into our humanness, we emerged from the womb to be born into this world.

As we emerged from the Lower Chamber, the womb, and began the long, arduous journey out into the world, we entered the next chamber, the Queen's Chamber. I had been given direction that this chamber represented the body—our earthly aspect. The ancient Egyptians viewed the body as the temple of the spirit, and for this principle the body was worshiped. The body was adorned, anointed, fed well, and treated well, so that it would be a good container or vessel for the spirit. In the Queen's Chamber we entered into a state of appreciation for our bodies and meditated to balance our energy centers so that we could experience an inner state of harmony.

The King's Chamber represented the spirit. This is where we could connect with our heavenly aspect and the divine source of all life. This is where we could remember where we truly came from: the formlessness of the absolute. The goal of our work in the King's Chamber was to fully embody the divine.

The night before we entered the Great Pyramid I asked for a dream that would give me information about our time there. The hotel where we stayed is near the base of the Great Pyramid, and I took in the visuals of this awesome structure before I went to sleep. I did receive a powerful dream that evening. In the dream my group was in the Queen's Chamber. There was a member in the group who was carrying a great deal of colorful, bejeweled brooches in her hands. She was so burdened with the weight and awkwardness of carrying the jewelry that she couldn't climb out of the Queen's Chamber and up the long, steep staircase to the King's Chamber. I instructed her to leave her jewelry behind. She refused. She had made the decision to stay in the Queen's Chamber and not journey to the King's Chamber so that she could hold on to these colorful jewels. In the dream I was shocked that anyone could make such a decision. The final message I received was that one could not go into the King's Chamber weighed down with earthly things, be they material objects or qualities associated with our humanness. This message had great meaning to me on many levels, and it connected with a spiritual vision I had had earlier.

Prior to leaving for Egypt, I had had a visitation by a spirit before I went to sleep. My eyes were open and I was awake, and at the same time I was fully aware of a great healing spiritual presence in my bedroom. This spirit temporarily took away all the pain and suffering I was carrying in my body. Being an empath, I tend to take on the pain and suffering of others, and recently I had been feeling very burdened by all the pain around me. This spirit gave me the physical experience of releasing all the pain I was carrying. I felt so light and so free. The feeling was divine—and unfamiliar, as taking on other people's pain has been a life issue for me. The spirit explained that I could not be a vessel for transmutation until I could let go of all the pain I had taken on from the suffering of humans and other life forms on earth. As the divine feels no pain, the bondage of the pain I carry prevents me from bringing through the divine energy needed for transmutation. The spirit explained to me that the qualities of being an empath actually prohibit one from being a healer. This experience directly related to the dream in which no one could get into the King's Chamber while weighed down.

As a teacher of spiritual healing since the early 1980s, I was shaken up by both the visitation and the dream. I understood the obvious message: that the weight of material possessions could obstruct the way to spiritual enlightenment. But I had always believed that being an empath, feeling what others feel in my own body and being, was a key to my ability as a spiritual healer.

Working with transmutation, it is important to understand the difference between compassion and empathy. At some point in your life and practice you have probably had a vision or perceived understanding of the divine mother. The Christian ethic leads us to believe that Mary took on the suffering of the world. This is not true. Mary and the other aspects of the divine mother, such as Isis and Kuan Yin, teach us about compassion. One can have compassion for someone's suffering without taking on his pain. This is one of the prevalent teachings of all the great mystics. You must have compassion for others' suffering to be a healer. The question you must ask is, can you be a healer while you are burdened by the pain of others? Can we bring through the divine love of the absolute while being weighed down by the feelings of others? The great mystics would say the answer to this is no. In our culture, this question might create great confusion.

There are stories of the ability of mystics to transmute poisons by actually ingesting them. In Hindu mythology, Shiva was known to ingest the poisons of the world and transmute them into healing energy. Shamans ingest and transmute poisons by being completely merged with their helping spirits. In this way the shaman is not hurt, for the spirits take the toxins and transmute them. Yes, this can be done. But one must journey past the process of empathy and make sure that the energies taken on are kept moving. The key here is the perception of pain. In order to take on pain or toxins and transmute them, one must perceive all pain and poison as merely an illusion.

As you proceed with these chapters, the concept should become clearer to you. It is important to truly understand the difference between compassion and empathy and the taking on of pain and poison to transmute them before stepping into the role of transmuter.

To finish the story of our night in the Great Pyramid: Before entering the king's chamber, we took off all jewelry and power objects and tried to let go of anything that would anchor us to our life on earth. The rest of the night we spent toning, dancing, and meditating as the space was created for each of us to connect with and embody the absolute. My experiences during this night gave me the words I needed to return home and finish writing this chapter.

This part of the book takes us into the ancient practices of the mystics who could perform the miracle of transmutation. We begin with the cross-cultural practice of dismemberment, used to dissolve the ego and earthly concerns that prevent us from remembering our connection to the source of life. From dismemberment we move on to transfiguration, shape-shifting into the aspects of divine that allow for transmutation to take place. We will move on to working with the healing power of words and sound as employed for transmutation. As we have learned from the Taoists, Hindus, Egyptians, and other mystical traditions as well as from David Bohm, representing the physics point of view, energy cannot be destroyed; nothing dies completely, but its nature can be changed, transmuted. We will look at the different modes of healing using sound, touch, visualization, and prayer.

15

Dismemberment

The process of dismemberment is a cross-cultural method of initiation as well as a spiritual practice used to deepen one's connection with the source of all life and remember the truth of one's nature and identity.

Dismemberment happens as a vision, which can come in a shamanic journey, a dream, or a meditation. In this vision one is literally dismembered by helping spiritual forces. A few examples of this might be where the initiate is chopped up, burned down to the bone, eaten by an animal, pecked down to the bone by birds, or stripped of skin and flesh by a sandstorm. The spirits can be quite creative, so these are just a few examples. Mircea Eliade, a scholar of shamanism, gives numerous examples of shamanic dismemberment in his book *Shamanism: Archaic Techniques of Ecstasy.*

The process sounds gruesome, but it actually marks an initiation into a spiritual path and practice and provides healing. In dismemberment you lose your ego and sense of self as well as all that weighs you down from experiencing your connection with the divine. As you lose your ego and allow your body, mind, and emotions to be devoured by spiritual forces, you are once again reunited with the source of all life, from which you came. Part I described creating a story that would put you in touch with the divine. Through singing, dancing, and meditation you learned how to become in union again with your creator. Dismemberment uses direct methods to accomplish the same goal. Everything that keeps you separate from your creator is devoured or stripped away, so you are once again formless, empty, pure spirit. In this way you remember the truth of your identity. All that surrounds your spirit is taken away. When you come back from this experience you remember the truth of who you are and where you came from. All that is ill is removed, and what is put back together is healthy and pure. Herein lies the healing component of dismemberment.

Michael Harner has made a deep pursuit of the practice of dismemberment as used for initiation, and in some of the advanced workshops on shamanism I teach through the Foundation for Shamanic Studies the participants are introduced to dismemberment journeys. I am always amazed at how in a dismemberment journey participants can reach the same enlightened state of consciousness and pure union with the divine creator that I and others have achieved through a near-death experience.

I am also amazed by how many people share with me in an introductory workshop in shamanic journeying that they had a journey of dismemberment without being formally introduced to it. Participants spontaneously report being ripped apart or eaten by a bear or some other powerful mammal or bird. No one has ever returned from a journey in a state of panic about this, as no pain or fear was experienced at the time. People have a sense that this is a sacred experience. Many participants in my workshops also report to me that they had dreams of dismemberment as children, which accords with the writings of Carl Jung, who saw dismemberment dreams as an initiation into a spiritual realm of knowledge.

In all traditions, dismemberment journeys or meditations are used not only as an initiation into a spiritual path, but as a way to deepen one's connection with the divine for the purposes of enlightenment and for healing. Dismemberment appears in the mythology of all major religions, showing that the egoic, self-possessed man must die and a new one be born. There are many levels to looking at the death and rebirth aspects of dismemberment, as they can even apply to the cycle of crops and nature, teaching us about the ebb and flow of life.

Let us look again at the Egyptian myth of the story of Osiris, Isis, and Horus. Osiris was dismembered by his brother Set and the pieces of his body scattered through the land. Isis gathered his pieces together. Osiris's body of matter was destroyed, but his spirit could not die. Isis transformed into her heavenly aspect of a bird to mate with him. As two spirits consummating their love, they birthed the holy child Horus.

In *The Unfolding Self* Ralph Metzner explains the shamanic dismemberment experience in the following way:

> Shamans may have visions in which they see and feel themselves being dismembered, or cut open, or flayed, or reduced to a skeleton. In some of the Australian aboriginal tribes, the would-be medicine man is symbolically "cut open" with stones; the abdominal organs are "removed" and replaced by crystals, which give him curing and clairvoyant power after he is put back together. In Siberia and among the Eskimos, the initiate is divested of flesh and contemplates his skeleton before being reassembled. In other cultures there may be a "stripping" of the skin, followed by its being washed or replaced by a new one. It is important that such apparently gruesome inner experiences are sought out by the shaman in training, for they are followed by a feeling and vision of the body being renewed and by the acquisition of magical or healing powers.[1]

It's interesting to note that when I facilitate students in a dismemberment journey, no instructions are given except to ask the helping spirits to dismember them. This is taught in advanced workshops, where participants are already grounded in the practice of shamanic journeying and know what sources of help are available to them. It is not uncommon for someone to have the experience of body organs being removed and crystals replacing them, as was seen among the Australian Aborigines, even if that person has no prior knowledge of the cross-cultural practice of dismemberment.

Dismemberment is used in Buddhist meditation as a regular spiritual practice; the transformative experience of dissolving the ego liberates one from the limitations of the mind. In Tibetan Buddhism this practice is known as the *chod,* where the goal is to break through the veil of *maya* that creates the illusion of separateness.[2]

In *Hidden Truths: Magic, Alchemy, and the Occult* Buddhist scholar Robert Thurman compares the dismemberment process in shamanism and the yogic traditions. The initiatory experiences of the shaman involve dismemberment and images of being dissolved. The yogic practice involves withdrawal from the gross physical body, which corresponds to the shaman's energy being separated from the senses, ego, and body. The subtle energy, once free, can explore the hidden universe and construct a new reality.[3]

One of the most prevalent dismemberment practices comes from the Hindu tradition. The goddess Kali, the divine mother of life, is known as the goddess of transformation and rules the process of transmutation. For Kali, life and death are the same. In *Tantric Yoga and the Wisdom Goddesses* David Frawley, who is recognized in both India and the West for his knowledge of Vedic teachings, describes Kali in her role of creator and destroyer. Before we can create the new, we must destroy the old. Time is both creation and destruction. It is only when we can allow our attachment to our material nature to be destroyed that our resurrection is possible. We sacrifice our identity, ego, and beliefs to the divine. Kali is the form of divine energy who accepts this sacrificial offering.

It is through this state of ego death that we can experience union with Kali and create and destroy the entire universe with our every breath, sensation, and thought. Death is not an end but the doorway to the eternal; therefore the death of the separate self brings us to eternal life.[4]

For many initiates on the tantric path, a path of transmutation, meditations of dismemberment, and giving oneself over to Kali is followed daily. This practice leads to such a level of ego dissolution that a spiritual master or guru is needed to guide initiates into this formless way of existence.

Kali is also often associated with the element of fire. Fire is known as the element of transmutation, while Kali is seen as the goddess of transmutation. Thus, the connection between these two forces is great. We give to Kali all in us that needs to be burned, all that keeps us separate from our own divinity. Fire's great healing and forging power provides the opportunity for transmutation.

We can even see the principle of dismemberment as talked about in alchemy. According to Manly Hall, the stages of alchemy can be traced back to the lives and activities of the world saviors and numerous mythologies such as Jesus dying upon the cross, Hiram at the west gates of the Temple, Orpheus on the banks of the river Hebros, Krishna on the banks of the Ganges, and Osiris. Alchemists understood the passage in the Bible that states, "Except that a man be born again, he cannot see the kingdom of God."

Jacob Boehme, a seventeenth-century mystic, defines the symbolism of the crucifixion as dismemberment. The cross represents life on earth and the crown of thorns the suffering of the soul within the physical body as well as the victory of the spirit over darkness. The naked body represents detachment from earthly things, and the body nailed to the cross describes the death of self-will—a reminder that man merely serves as an instrument so that divine will can be executed.[5] Once again working with this symbolism, we see the theme of sacrificing the part of man that experiences himself as separate so that the universal consciousness may be liberated.[6]

There is even a story that comes from the Taoist teachings of

Chuang Tzu, as described in *The Relaxation Response* by Dr. Herbert Benson:

> Yen Hui said, "I have made some progress."
>
> "What do you mean?" asked Confucius
>
> "I have forgotten humanity and righteousness," replied Yen Hui.
>
> "Very good, but that is not enough," said Confucius.
>
> On another day Yen Hui saw Confucius again and said, "I have made some progress."
>
> "What do you mean?" asked Confucius.
>
> "I have forgotten ceremonies and music," replied Yen Hui.
>
> "Very good, but that is not enough," said Confucius.
>
> Another day Yen Hui saw Confucius again and said, "I have made some progress."
>
> "What do you mean?" asked Confucius.
>
> Yen Hui said, "I forget everything while sitting down."
>
> Confucius' face turned pale. He said, "What do you mean by sitting down and forgetting everything?"
>
> "I cast aside my limbs," replied Yen Hui, "discard my intelligence, detach from both body and mind, and become one with the Great Universal (Tao). This is called sitting down and forgetting everything."
>
> Confucius said, "When you become one with the Great Universal, you will have no partiality, and when you are part of the process of transformation, you will have no constancy. You are really a worthy man. I beg to follow your steps."[7]

As you can see, the practice and process of dismemberment is universal in clearing away and dissolving all the aspects of our humanness, of our earthly selves, that keep us from remembering our connection with the divine and source from which we came. This is essential as we call down and call forth the heavenly spiritual aspects of the divine to heal the earth through transmutation. We must remember our true nature as we call forth the true nature of life and purity from the natural world around us.

The two things that separate us from the divinity necessary to embody the absolute for the purpose of transmutation are our perception of separateness and our limiting belief systems. When you really come down to the core of what prevents you from creating miracles, you will most likely find that you don't believe you can do it. The rational and scientific part of ourselves cannot embrace such a notion. Ask yourself this question: Do you really believe that you can transmute polluted water into holy water? I am sure the desire is there, but is the belief there? In some spiritual practices a form of dismemberment is used where you give up your head to the spiritual forces that you work with; this represents giving up the limited views and the mental chatter of the logical mind.

In our culture, where we don't consciously work with the spiritual practice of dismemberment, we find the universe providing us with some literal examples of this. People who lose everything that they think is important to them in a disaster such as an earthquake, hurricane, or fire often find a deeper meaning to the preciousness of life. They often realize that the material objects lost are just distractions from the important aspects of life. People faced with a life-threatening situation often remember what is truly important to them—what life has to offer. The things that distract us from a higher power or the divine are often stripped away so that we may remember our true nature. We might make the choice to work with this on a more conscious level rather than having some type of dismemberment forced upon us.

○ EXERCISES

It is important to understand that dismemberment is an initiation into a new perception and will impact your life on many levels. I have chosen to present a visualization you can use to get the experience of dismemberment. As all the exercises in this book are optional, you need to decide whether or not you would like to have this experience. Please honor where you are in your own process.

Typically the dismemberment process would be more of a spontaneous vision, but use what I provide to get you started.

I would suggest that you tape this visualization or have someone else read it to you. It will be hard to get into the experience if you are trying to read it for yourself. Before beginning this exercise, get into a relaxed state. Do this where you will not disturbed by the phone or doorbell ringing or someone walking into the room.

To begin, take a few deep breaths. Close your eyes while continuing to breathe. Let your breath connect with your heartbeat, your life force. Listen to the sound of your heart. Allow your awareness to drift from your body and the room you are in. You almost feel as if you could float.

Imagine yourself being transported to some beautiful place in nature where you can connect with the elements of the natural world. Let yourself go to some favorite place that has a body of water. Listen to the sound of the water. Walk up to it and touch it. Feel the temperature. With your eyes closed, feel the air around you, the earth beneath you, and the power of the sun above you. Connect deeply with these great sources of power and life. Open your eyes in this imaginary place and look around you. Take in the colors and the smells. What is the sky above you like? What is the plant and animal life sharing this space with you?

Reach your arms up to the sky and plant your feet on the earth. You become aware of a great wind swirling around you. The wind becomes so strong that you are forced to close your eyes. It rips at your body, whereupon your skin, bones, and every bit of your matter dissolve to sand. There is nothing left of you, no body, no mind, just pure consciousness.

Your consciousness begins to move up toward the sky, traveling farther than the clouds and sun, through the stars, through the planets and all the galaxies. As pure consciousness, you have no awareness of self; you are one with all. You are the stars, the galaxies, the great dark void that is the place of unlimited possibilities. You have not died, yet you have not been born. You are empty, yet at the same time you are full. As pure consciousness, you travel to a great light. This light has no color, yet shines. It does not speak, but it is pure being. The light does not recognize you as separate from it, but embraces you and breathes pure love. Radiance flows through the universe. You become one with this radiance. You are radiance, you are love, you are pure being. Experience that.

Then in a flicker of time there is a thought. With that thought a pulsation comes. Still as pure consciousness, you begin to separate from this great radiant light. As a fleck of this light, you have a thought: What would it be like to have a form that could embody this great light? This leads to more thoughts: What would it be like to dance as this light? What would it be like to touch as this light? What would it be like to taste as this light? What would it be like to smell as this light? What would it be like to manifest thought and spirit into form as this light?

These thoughts of wonder lead to movement. You become aware that you are moving away from this great light. You are once again moving down through galaxies and stars. You stop. Thought has led to awareness; awareness has led to thought. Which comes first, you just don't know, nor do you care. You are still a being of light, but now with a destiny. What is your destiny? Why are you returning to earth? What is it that you want to experience on this earthly plane? It has something to do with experiencing your divinity while in a body that can have feelings and sensations. Consider this for some time.

You remember. You remember the source of your life and the decision you made to have an earthly experience. You put your attention toward the earth. It's such a beautiful planet. It has so many lovely elements and life forms to interact with. It is pure spirit transformed into manifest being. Earth is alive. It has a pulse, a heartbeat. It has a pulse just like the great light from which you came. The two pulses are in harmony; the beat and vibration are one and the same. The light is formless but alive. The earth has form and pulses like the light. There is a great light that lives in the earth. You are aware of it. The light above is also in the earth below.

You go closer and closer until you enter the earth's gravitational pull. Then in the same way the contents of an hourglass slip effortlessly into the lower portion of the vessel, you slip back into your body. You are once again standing in this great place in nature. You open your eyes in this place. Your arms and hands are still reaching toward the sun. The bright light of the sun is you. Your feet are planted on the earth; you are the earth. You are aware that you are the plants and flowers, the trees, the animals, the water, and the air. The sense of being separate is just a perception. In truth, there is no separation. You are one with the divine source from which you came, and you came to experience that divinity in a life form that perceives itself separate from the all but in reality is the one. There is only one pulse, there is only one heartbeat. And your heartbeat is in harmony with the one.

From this place of knowing and remembering, you make a conscious choice that you will remember this experience. You will take back the knowing of your true nature to the world that you now inhabit.

You take in the beauty of this place one more time. And with your breath and intention you make a decision to leave this imaginary place and return fully to your body, resting in your room. You start to bring your awareness back into your body. You wiggle your toes and touch with your fingers the floor, chair, or bed you are sitting or lying on. You smell the air in this room. You listen to the sounds around you. You breathe deeply and open your eyes. You sit quietly, reflecting on your experience of merging with the source of all life. You remember your divine nature. You embody divinity, light, and love. And you stay with that until you are ready to leave this room and rejoin your life once again, remembering that everything you perceive around you as separate is merely an illusion. You decide that you will always remember the divinity in you and all things around you, and you will honor the spirit in all things.

Start a daily practice of visualizing or experiencing yourself giving up your head to the spiritual helpers, gods, goddesses, or aspect of the divine you work with. Begin by asking yourself this question: Do you believe that you have the power to create a miracle? If the answer is yes, you are done for the day. If the answer is no, give up the part of yourself that limits your unlimited potential to transmute yourself and the earth.

16

Transfiguration

I planted the seeds to write *Medicine for the Earth* in 1998, before I left for my first spiritual pilgrimage to Egypt. A few days after I returned from this trip I had a very powerful dream. The Egyptian god Anubis came to me and introduced himself in the dream as the god that guarded the levels between the worlds. He told me that the missing piece to my work with transmutation was transfiguration.

I had never heard this word before. When I woke up I asked my husband if he had ever heard the word *transfiguration.* He said he thought it had to do with shape-shifting. I immediately got out of bed and went to the dictionary. Indeed, *transfiguration* meant "shape-shifting." In my work with shamanism I was very familiar with the concept of shape-shifting. I had heard many tales of shamans being able to shape-shift into the form of animals. But I could not figure out what this had to do with transmutation.

As I held the question, the path was quickly revealed to me. A client of mine who was a devout Christian led me to material on the transfiguration of Jesus before he performed many of his healing miracles.

The New Testament has a passage in which Jesus took Peter, James, and John to a high mountain, where Jesus transfigured before them: "His face shone as the sun and his garments became white as snow." Other accounts of this same phenomenon say the clothes of Jesus became dazzlingly white, whiter than any bleached garment. There are accounts of miraculous healings when sick people touched the hem of Jesus's garment while he was in this illumined state.

Ron Roth uses the term "resurrection current" to refer to the energy running through Jesus when he transfigured into divine light. The resurrection current became a channel for healing the sick and producing miracles. It is through our union with the divine that we can transfigure, experiencing ourselves aglow with the spirit of God.[1]

There are endless accounts of mystics and religious figures transfiguring into light. In *The Unfolding Self* Ralph Metzner describes the account of a German traveler who visited Ramana Maharshi and observed his transfiguration. The traveler watched as Ramana's brown face transformed, becoming luminous as he radiated with a light from within.[2] In *Krishnamurti: 100 Years* Evelyne Blau cites a student who was shocked to see the small, slender figure of Krishnamurti change right in front of her very eyes to a tall, luminescent figure that looked like the Buddha. His luminosity affected all who were in his presence.[3] Similar eyewitness accounts are told of the Indian saint Ramakrishna as well as the spiritual master Sai Baba.

Larry Peters, who is an anthropologist and a psychologist as well as an initiated shaman in the Tibetan tradition, says that for shamans and mystics, light is a transcendent experience and not a metaphor. In the Judeo-Christian tradition creation begins with "Let there be light." Krishna is described as "brighter than a thousand suns," and Christ is called "the light of the world." Saints are often portrayed with a nimbus and transfigure into luminous beings. After dismemberment, Eskimo shamans are filled with light, giving them their psychic and healing abilities. During initiatory experiences of the Aboriginal shamans a luminous quartz crystal is placed in their body by the celestial great god, allowing them flight to heaven. Experiences of being transformed by light is spoken of among shamans in Siberia, Malaysia, and North and South America. Mircea Eliade adds to this by saying that an experience of light changes human existence by creating a spiritual rebirth, opening one to the world of spirit.[4]

Ralph Metzner, in *The Unfolding Self,* shares a story about the well-known explorer Rasmussen quoting an Eskimo shaman as saying, "Every real shaman has to feel *qaumaneq,* a light within the body, inside his head or brain, something that gleams like fire, that enables him to see in the dark, and with closed eyes see into things which are hidden, and also into the future."[5]

In transfiguration and transmutation, it is not just enough to encounter luminosity; the key is to embody that luminosity. This is the energy of radiance that Jack Schwarz speaks of that allows for miraculous healings to take place, as well as the energy that fuels the miraculous healings and manifestations that mystics such as Sai Baba can perform.

In the dismemberment visualization I led you through, I didn't just take you to the light; I had you become the light of the absolute. Dismemberment is a practice that can take us back to the source so that we can remember our true identity. The next step is to embody the luminosity of the divine through transfiguration while you are here.

In working with the principle of divine intervention, we know that the intermediary spirits of the divine have the power to heal and to create miracles. People have reported having visions where they are healed by religious saints, and we also have many accounts of people being healed by the helping spirits encountered in shamanic journeys. Through my own experience as well as reports from clients and students, I find it is common for a power animal or teacher in human form to show up in a journey or dream and provide a healing. I have seen chronic and painful conditions plaguing clients simply be cured by intervention of the spirits alone.

I had a student whose father was dying of cancer. The father was a very conservative and religious man who under ordinary circumstances would never consider shamanic journeying. As he was dealing with enormous pain, though, he agreed to give it a try. He met a power animal who proceeded to take away all of his pain. The man was able to stop and stay off all his pain medication. His power animal kept him pain free and helped him to live his remaining years peacefully.

In *Welcome Home* I shared how in a dream I was healed of a very painful condition. I had an illness that was not life-threatening but was the cause of chronic pain. I was living in San Francisco at the time, and I consulted with every specialist I could find, but I was told that I just had to learn to live with my situation. Months went by, and I was desperate for help. I had tried every alternative treatment, gone to psychics, had people journey for me—I had left no stone unturned. Nothing worked, and I was becoming very depressed at the thought of facing a future full of pain. I started praying for a healing dream before I went to sleep at night. I asked every night, as there was nothing left for me to try except prayer. Finally, after a month of asking, I was blessed with a dream that would cure my condition. A young Native American man stepped out from behind my couch. He said, "You have a pain right there," pointing to the part of my body that hurt. Next he took out a translucent blue rattle made of a material I am unfamiliar with and shook it over my pain. In the dream I felt my pain leave. My healing dream was twenty years ago, and there has been no pain since.

Based on the phenomenon of divine intervention, in your transfiguration you could also take the form of the spirits, saints, or mystics who have the ability to heal. One could transfigure into a power animal or spiritual teacher to provide healing for people, animals, plants, trees, and the environment.

An example of this type of dismemberment/transfiguration comes from a student of mine in a workshop. In her journey she was taken by a crow to the top of a volcano, where he used wild-grape vine to tie her to a cross-shaped wooden frame. She was then dismembered by being pecked to pieces by a bunch of crows and vultures. When all of her flesh was gone, the crows lifted her bones and threw them into the volcano. She then sank slowly through the molten lava to the bottom, where she slid through a small opening carrying her to the outside. As she emerged she became a white wolf.

She had an extraordinary sense of power and could hardly contain herself from jumping up and bounding around the room. Her shoulders were very strong, and her gait was swift and sure. She experienced herself as a wolf, magnificent to behold. She could see herself protecting her young, leading the pack, able to track and hunt whatever was needed to feed her circle.

After experiencing her wolfness for a while, she returned to her power animal, turtle, to tell what happened. Her entrance into the earth, which is a cave, was decorated with flowers for celebration. As she wanted to offer thanks, she brought incense, tobacco, and more flowers and danced with powerful leaps and strides. She described her experience as amazingly joyous.

At this point turtle asked the woman to lie beneath her, and a medicine wheel of light was burned into the woman's chest. She thanked the spirits who helped her, and prepared to leave. As she left the journey she returned to the room with wolf as part of her. On her return she still felt filled with power; her hands were vibrating and full of energy. She was able to share some of the energy when the session closed with the group holding hands. Afterward she found herself overcome with emotion, crying with joy, gratitude, and awe.

Since then she does feel different and more wolflike. She is physically stronger. Mentally and emotionally she feels focused and power-filled.

Ammachi is an Indian saint who lives in southern India. Every year she travels around the United States, where thousands of people witness her miracles of healing through transfiguration. Through her spiritual practice she becomes the embodiment of the divine mother. There's a story of Ammachi sucking the illness out of the sores of a leper. Once someone has transfigured into a divine state, the illusion of separateness and belief that a substance can be harmful is dissolved. In this state, Ammachi has been known to turn water into milk. She is an example of what can be accomplished when one fully embodies the divine.

Another aspect of transfiguration involves moving from an earthly aspect into a heavenly aspect. Isis transfigured from her earthly, human aspect to her heavenly aspect of a bird to remember Osiris and birth the holy child Horus into being. Horus has his earthly form but also appears as the falcon. Thoth, the god of wisdom, often shows himself in his heavenly form—a baboon. Hathor, the goddess of love and beauty, is depicted as a cow, and Anubis, the god that guards the gateways between the worlds, appears as the jackal in his heavenly aspect.

In the process of transfiguration we must raise our vibration higher than the vibration we embrace in the gross material world. We cannot be weighed down by material and earthly concerns. If you are too dense, you cannot transfigure. This is where dismemberment and the other spiritual practices I have suggested come into play. You must be able to move into a divine state of awareness to transfigure and leave your ego, desires, and mental constructs behind.

By transfiguring into divine light and love, spiritual intermediaries, or the heavenly aspects of ourselves, we can bring through the luminosity needed for the transmutation of pollution in our world.

There is another aspect of transfiguration that we need to look at. Some spiritual masters have not just transfigured themselves, but also transfigured a substance in order to heal. For example, one could bring the divine through to water to become holy water, which can heal. There is holy water in many of the healing sites around the world.

In *The Search for Omm Sety* Dorothy Eady describes the pool of water called the Osiron, which emanated light at the temple of Abydos in Egypt. The head of Osiris is supposed to be buried here.

She shares how she witnessed many people touching this water to parts of the body that needed healing, and being cured. Now this pool of water suffers severe pollution. I contend that this pool can once again be imbued with the power of the divine.

Many people make spiritual pilgrimages to the Santuario de Chimayo in New Mexico, where in the chapel there is a hole filled with soil that has been imbued with the power of the divine. In this place, too, many miraculous healings are reported by people who place the soil on their body.

There is a story that comes from accounts of followers of Sai Baba about how he once suffered paralysis in his legs through being poisoned. His followers went into a panic and tried to convince him to see a neurosurgeon. One of his followers was a doctor who tested him and watched over him. One day Sai Baba declared, "I am tired of this." At this point he reached into a tumbler of water, sprinkling it on one of his legs. The leg straightened out and was healed. The doctor in the room asked if he could do this. Sai Baba told him he could if he was given the power. Sai Baba transferred power to the doctor, who put his fingers in the tumbler of water and sprinkled water on the other crippled leg. His other leg straightened out and was healed.[6] In this case, I believe the water was blessed with the power of the divine and was transmuted into healing and holy water.

I will share more on this in Part VI, "Ceremonies for Transmutation."

You can incorporate the practice of transfiguration into your daily life. Many of the students who I have taught to journey for transfiguration have found there are times when invoking a divine state in their ordinary life is helpful. For example, if you find yourself in a challenging situation at work or with a loved one then through intention you can embody a compassionate divine force that can transmute the energy of the situation.

Using the principle "As above, so below; as within, so without," I suggest bringing through the divine that lives inside of you. Calling forth your own divinity invokes light, love, and compassion, which serve as "healing medicine" for the earth and ourselves.

A note of caution is that you need a healthy ego to do this. You don't want to see yourself as Jesus or other religious figures. Part of walking the razor's edge of your spiritual path is not losing your identity as well as being able to change your state of consciousness at will.

It is well known in shamanism that shamans cross back and forth between the worlds at will. The difference between a shaman and a psychotic is that the shaman crosses at will and a psychotic gets stuck being unaware of the reality he is in.

To be successful in your spiritual practice and healing the earth you must be able to engage and disengage with divine forces at will.

O Exercises

As with dismemberment, please think about whether you want to proceed with the exercises in transfiguration. Take responsibility for where you are spiritually and emotionally in your life. If you do the remainder of the exercises in this book, omitting the exercises of dismemberment and transfiguration, you will still find that your life transforms in a powerful way. The exercises on transfiguration are developed for people who have been committed to spiritual practices for a long period of time.

Now that I have given you a visualization for dismemberment, it is time to create your own. You have seen the purpose of dismemberment: to lose the parts of the self that block you from being in a divine state. Use whatever elements feel right to you. Use the elements of other exercises in this book to create the sacred space to support the depth of your experience.

From the dismembered state you want to experience transfiguration. You can experiment with embodying the divine light when you return from your dismemberment, or you might wish to embody the power animal, religious figure, or spiritual teacher you work with.

You want the experience of this for just a short period of time as you learn to work with this energy. I would suggest no more than fifteen minutes at first. The duration will depend on your spiritual practice, your spiritual foundation, and your level of concentration. If you are being introduced to spiritual practices through this book, take it slowly. I truly believe that "slow and steady wins the race."

You might allow your dismemberment and transfiguration experience to occur during a short piece of music that supports your meditative state of consciousness. Or you can set an alarm clock that has a gentle alarm or comes on with music. You don't want to be shocked out of your experience, as you may be disoriented and feel ungrounded. The cure for this is to go back into your experience and silently talk yourself back into the room and your body. Sitting out in nature with the intention of wanting to ground will provide just that. If you can't get to a place in nature, visualize yourself sitting with a tree, rooting yourself into the earth and your body as a tree does.

> When you have had the experience of transfiguration for a few minutes, slowly return to the room and your body. You can use the way I brought you out of the dismemberment, or you can use whatever method that you are accustomed to when returning from a meditative state.
>
> You can also experience transfiguration while chanting or toning and calling down and forth the divine.
>
> This experience will enable you to perform the work in the next part of the book on transmuting the water you drink, the food you eat, the air you breathe, and the body and earth you inhabit. Light and love heal, if we can embody these energies completely.

We have looked at the heavenly aspects of the gods and goddesses of ancient Egypt. Now it is time for you to tap into the heavenly aspect of yourself. Using the meditative methods from previous exercises or your own methods of accessing spiritual information, ask to be shown your own heavenly aspect of the divine. One level of this will be light, and you can choose to stop there. But there are other intermediary aspects of the divine. If you choose to work with one of these, what would that look like to you? What are the qualities, gifts, and strengths that go along with this heavenly aspect of yourself?

Once again, you can transfigure from your human earthly form to this heavenly form when you work with the process of transmutation.

To heal the earth through transmutation:

You must remember that feelings of separation from the
divine and other beings are all an illusion. To reestablish
your connection with the divine as well as all life around
you, call forth the divine in all the polluted elements of the
earth.
You must transfigure into the divine and absolute power of
the universe.

Parts of the formula for transmutation used here:

Intention: By holding the intention to remember your
connection with source and let the divine shine through,
you can dissolve the ego and transfigure into the energy
needed for transmutation to occur.
Love: Love is all that exists when we realize the duality of life is
just an illusion. The divine aspect needed for
transmutation embodies love.
Harmony: Death and rebirth shapes you into a life form that
embraces harmony as you remember your connection
with all life. You must be in a spiritual and emotional state
of harmony to embody and transfigure into the divine,
embodying its luminescence.
Union: Dismemberment and transfiguration are union with
the absolute.
Focus: You must hold your attention and focus to the
intention of wanting to radiate luminescence.

Concentration: You must concentrate on the practices that allow you to have the transformative experiences of death, rebirth, and transfiguration.

Imagination: You must be able to imagine the heavenly aspects in you and around you.

17

The Power of Sound and Words

The knower of the mystery of sound knows the mystery of the whole universe.
—SUFI MASTER HAZRAT INAYAT KHAN

Sound heals, and words create the magic of physical manifestation. These are concepts that we can learn from spiritual traditions worldwide. I have already touched on the subject of the use of chants and mantras, and we know from the research of people such as Don Campbell and Robert Gass that chanting has the ability to heal.

Although recently rediscovered in the West, the concept that sound can heal has been known since the beginning of time. The Vedic chants and mantras of the yogis and the chants of the shamans from Siberia, other parts of Asia, northern Europe, North and South America, and Africa have long been used for the transmutation of illness and toxins. Robert Gass writes about mystics' fascination with harmonics, which occur in precise mathematical series. He says the healing and spiritual power of the harmonics of sound can be seen as "the light in music."[1] He also adds that one of the definitions of the word *healing* is "to make sound."[2]

The Hindu scriptures teach us that *aum* is the sacred syllable from which the entire universe was manifested. Prayers of the Christians, Hebrews, and Moslems end with the word *amen*, and Daniel Reid, a leading Western authority on traditional Chinese medicine and Taoist healing practices, states in *Harnessing the Power of the Universe* that scholars believe *amen* is a direct derivative of this ancient Sanskrit syllable.[3] Ahmed Abdelmawgood Fayed, Egyptologist and lecturer, says that for the Hebrews, Moslems, and Christians, the translation of *amen* is "the invisible god." Herein lies the connection.

We have looked at how our attitudes and thoughts shape our world. It is time for us to work with the power of words so that transmutation of pollution may occur. Words have always been used to shape the formless into physical manifestation. In most of the world's religions, creation began with the spoken word. Genesis says that God created the world with the words "Let there be light." The New Testament says, "In the beginning was the Word and the Word was with God and the Word was God" (John 1:1). We also saw this to be true in the Egyptian myths of creation.

Robert Gass shares more examples of the use of sound to create. The Greek god Orpheus brought forth form through magical singing. In the cosmology of the Hopi, the sun god and earth goddess chant life into being. African, Australian, Polynesian, and Japanese creation myths all include the belief that matter and life are formed through God's sounds.[4]

The ancients took the power of word very seriously. In the Sanskrit language every syllable and vowel voiced is thought to set up a vibration that goes out into the universe and returns as a physical manifestation. One Hindu creation story tells that the world sprang forth from the skulls of Kali's necklace, where each skull is a letter of the Sanskrit alphabet.[5] The ancient Egyptians believed that every word had magical power, and great caution was used before speaking words. They knew that certain arrangements of words could create an energy in the universe influencing physical matter. Metaphor was used in place of certain words, so as not to use the word itself; otherwise there would be an immediate manifestation.

The Egyptian Book of the Dead states that numerous words in the

Egyptian language could be translated as "magic." The most common of these words is *heka,* whose Coptic equivalent became the Greek word *mageia. Heka* has many translations, but its most important sense has to do with the power of words. In Egyptian magic, action and words were often the same thing.[6]

Jean Houston says that consciousness is created by naming. For ancient people, the word preceded all creation. Once something was named, it had a life and could be known. This underlies the Egyptian notion of *heka.*[7]

Caroline Casey, in *Making the Gods Work for You,* quotes the medieval philosopher Nicolas of Cusa: "If we understood the real name of even one thing in creation—we would understand the mind of God."[8]

Using words, chants, and mantras, the Egyptians and Hindus could transmute pain and illness. According to Michael Harner, the shamans of South America and the Sami shamans of Lapland and Norway have a tradition of using words to invoke healing. He talks about "word doctoring" among the Sami people, who have words or phrases to heal illnesses such as headaches.

Once again the Bible provides many examples of Jesus healing people through the use of words, declaring them healed. Moses commanded the parting of the Red Sea through the use of words, allowing the Jews to escape from Egypt. Magical incantations have been used by the Druid traditions of Europe for healing and creation.

Words and thought forms create a vibration that goes far into the universe, creating musical notes. We need to look at whether we send out harmonious notes into the universe, which in turn create harmony, or whether we send out disharmonious notes, creating chaos and illness. We call down the powers of the divine and call into being with our words. In the introduction and in Part III, I used the metaphor of seeing words as seeds that are planted. The seeds planted will decide what kind of plant grows.

We rarely pay attention to the power of the words we use. In our ignorance we end up calling into being a great deal of chaos and pollution. We do the same with our thought forms. If the divine created us in its own image and the divine is perfect, then we are perfect. If we say things about ourselves that are against our perfection, we move out of harmony with the divine inside and outside us, which can cause illness. For example, if you say that you are not good enough or if you believe you are not worthy, your words are out of harmony with divine creation.

You must work on bringing your words and thoughts back into a song of harmony. Without this harmony there can be no union. Without harmony and union there can be no transmutation. The universe sings glorious harmonious notes. Is the song of your life and beliefs harmonious?

○ EXERCISES

It is time to explore the energy and vibration behind the words you use. Journey or meditate on a word that holds energy for you. Write this word down. Read it and think about it through the day. Notice the vibration that comes out of this word.

For example, the word I began this process with is *brilliance.* When I meditated on and repeated this word to myself throughout the day, I could perceive the magical vibration this word creates. As I continued with this process I became so attached to the word *harmony* that I named my car Harmony.

Keep a list of words that you hear, read, or think of that have magical energy behind them.

Notice how when you move into a negative state of consciousness your thoughts and words no longer hold a positive vibration that is sent out. Think of what effect the murkiness of energy and vibration sent out will be reflected back in your life as well as how it affects the health of the earth.

Imagine your life as a garden. What seed words do you want to plant, nurture, and watch grow? Choose your seed words carefully.

As you begin to notice the energy and vibration of words, be more conscious of the words you use in your conversations with others. Think about what you are calling down for yourself and others. Think about what plant will grow out of the words you planted.

To heal the earth through transmutation, you must speak to yourself and others with words that create a vibration of love, harmony, and union with the divine. With words you can decree that pollution be reversed.

Parts of the formula for transmutation used here:

Intention: Words create the intention to heal or create illness.

Love: Words that have the power to heal embrace the vibration of love. Love heals.

Harmony: Harmonious notes sent out into the universe will create harmony reflected back to you in your life and the environment.

Union: Where there is harmony, there is union. Union is the energy behind transmutation.

Focus: You must have a strong focus to create the intention to use healing words.

Concentration: It takes a great deal of concentration to be aware of the words you use in your self-talk and your conversations with others.

Imagination: You must be able to imagine the energy and vibration that is sent out with the words you use.

18

The Power of Appreciation and Gratefulness

One of the most powerful methods I know of for transmutation is to understand the magic of appreciation. When we are in a state of appreciation and gratefulness, a veil lifts, revealing a state of perfection and divinity. This key can easily be overlooked. We give so much power to techniques, and we deny the power of simply changing our perception and state of consciousness as a driving force in transmutation. Perception is a key to everything. How you perceive your situation can be a tool for transmutation.

In this part of the book I have introduced you to the concept of dissolving your sense of self to unite with the source of life and embody the divine, which creates transmutation. You can transmute by bringing light and love into your body through transfiguration and through the laying on of hands. You can transmute using the power of sound by chanting and the magic of words and prayer. Transmutation can occur simply through a state of observation, as we have learned from Krishnamurti and David Bohm, or you can transmute using your imagination to visualize and experience with all your senses a perfect and divine environment devoid of pollution.

Without a state of consciousness that embraces appreciation, I don't think you will be successful with any of these methods. It is your body that contains the divine energy, whether you call it down from above or call it forth from within. Herein lies the metaphor of the ancient Egyptians perceiving the body as a temple. It is the temple for the divine. To be able to use the body to emanate luminescence and transmute through touch, sound, prayer, and visualization, you must be in deep appreciation for your body. In order to transmute what is ill in your life, you must be in a state of appreciation for life. To transmute environmental pollution, you must embody appreciation for the earth, the elements, and all of life.

Appreciation, honoring, and *gratefulness* are magical words that empower your ability to transmute. In Part II we worked with identifying what invokes the memory that life is precious. Now we must work with what we appreciate and why.

O EXERCISES

The key in our work here is to change our perception of our world, which in itself transforms our world. To transmute pollution in our body and on the earth we must appreciate and give thanks to everything that composes our body and our world. To work with this, you need to create time in your daily schedule and make this a daily spiritual practice. I will give you some suggestions of what you might be appreciative of, but you might add some things of your own. Please remember to give thanks for all that you are appreciating.

I appreciate the water around me and the rain that comes from above for _____

I appreciate the air I breathe for _____

I appreciate the earth I inhabit for _____

I appreciate the sun and light that comes through the earth and down from the sun for _____

I appreciate the living beings (the plants, the trees, the rocks, the animals, the insects, etc.), which share this great planet with me, for _____

I appreciate the food I eat for _____

I appreciate my feet as they _____

I appreciate my legs as they _____

I appreciate my trunk as it _____

I appreciate my arms as they _____

I appreciate my hands as they _____

I appreciate my neck and shoulders as they _____

I appreciate my head as it _____

I appreciate my eyes as they _____

I appreciate my nose as it _____

I appreciate my mouth, tongue, teeth, and throat as they _____

I appreciate my skin as it _____

I appreciate my nails as they _____

I appreciate my hair as it _____

I appreciate my brain as it _____

I appreciate my heart as it _____

I appreciate my lungs as it _____

I appreciate my liver as it _____

I appreciate my stomach as it _____

I appreciate my kidneys as they _____

I appreciate my pancreas as it _____

I appreciate my chest/breasts as they _____

I appreciate my male/female organs as they _____

I appreciate my blood as it _____

I appreciate my endocrine system as it _____

I appreciate my nerves as they _____

I appreciate my bones as they _____

I appreciate my joints and cartilage as they _____

I appreciate my spine as it _____

I appreciate my cells as they _____

I appreciate my DNA as it _____

I appreciate my friends and community for _____

I appreciate my coworkers for _____

The Power of Appreciation and Gratefulness *209*

I appreciate my job for _____

I appreciate my house for _____

I appreciate my creator for _____

I am in deep appreciation for my life for _____

Do this every day, even when you are depressed, anxious, angry, or frustrated. Work especially on parts of your body where you need healing. When you bump up against something you cannot appreciate, your awareness is raised to where there is disharmony in your life and beliefs.

Whenever you are afraid of losing something, be it your health, home, etc., you can reframe your fear by moving into a state of deep appreciation for what you fear you may lose.For example, if you are afraid of losing your home to a natural disaster, focus your thoughts on how much you appreciate your home. If you are afraid of losing your health, change your thoughts to how grateful you are for your healthy body.

Keep working. Doing this practice will bring light to all the dark places inside you. We often say to reach deep inside yourself to find your strength. Now I suggest you reach inside yourself to find your light. When you bring light through to yourself and to your life, transmutation is the only result possible.

You heal the earth through transmutation when you focus and remain in a state of deep appreciation and thankfulness, bringing light to all the dark places on earth.

Parts of the formula for transmutation used here:

Intention: If you hold the intention that you are grateful, your personal world and the world around you will transform in a beautiful way.

Love: Appreciation is a state of love. Love creates transmutation.

Harmony: When you are in a state of appreciation, you move into harmony with yourself and the divine forces in and around you.

Union: Appreciation brings you to a state of union with the source of all life. Where there is union there is transmutation.

Focus: Holding your intention to be in a state of constant appreciation takes focusing on your vision.

Concentrate: You must be able to concentrate on the focus of your intention.

Imagination: You must be able to imagine yourself in a place of appreciation for everything and imagine the transformation that can occur by embodying this state of being.

More to Think About

19

THE ONLY SAFE PLACE IS INSIDE YOU

We have been programmed genetically to try to survive. Therefore, when a catastrophe occurs, or if we think we are in danger, there is a biological drive to try to find safety. As biological beings, we spend a great deal of time and energy trying to create a safe world for ourselves.

Many years ago, there was a prediction that Los Angeles was going to suffer a devastating earthquake. Many people went into a panic and left the state. The roads were crowded and all airline flights were sold out. During this time a group of Tibetan Buddhist monks flew to Los Angeles to be on the land and pray. The message they brought with them was that when it looks like there is going to be trouble somewhere, don't leave but rather gather together with others and send positive thoughts so that the catastrophe won't occur. Although I heard that story over twenty years ago, the message has stayed with me.

Recently, fires started raging in New Mexico. This was a major catastrophe as the destruction to the land and homes was great. As Los Alamos Lab was in the wake of the fire, there was fear about the radiation that would leak into the air, especially because of the amount of radioactive waste that was buried in areas around the lab. Many people chose to leave New Mexico.

I wonder, however, where there is a safe place on the planet to go to. The truth is that as long as we have a body, we are always in physical danger. There is no safe place to go except inside ourselves, where we can tap into the truth of who we are. We are spirit, and in this sense we can never die.

If our house is in the path of a fire, yes we must leave. But when we are afraid of perceived danger that might come, I feel that the best solution is not to panic but to sit and be very still. Otherwise, we are swept away in a chaotic energy where solutions cannot be shown. We must gather together with other members from our community to focus our intention and concentrate our energies to bring forth harmony to the situation. As a community working together spiritually, we can provide the energy required to work with the forces of nature instead of battling these forces. As a community, we can create the sacred space necessary that allows the transmutation of toxins to occur.

Experiencing change on all levels is part of the human condition. We cannot run from or avoid change. We can, however, discover that home and safety live within; we can learn how to stay centered in the midst of great change; and we can realize that when we gather our spiritual energy together with others, we can create harmony within and harmony without.

WHEN YOU THINK YOUR TRANSMUTATION EFFORTS HAVE FAILED

In this book, I focus on the miracles that can occur when you change your state of perception and consciousness and embark on a path of spiritual practices. But sometimes even with the best intentions your efforts might seem to fail.

The first place I would look when your attempts fail is your belief system. A key to this work is having belief and faith in the power of the divine outside as well as the divine inside to create the miracle of healing and transmutation. As Jesus said: "If thou can believe, all things are possible." He taught that even having faith the size of a mustard seed was enough to work miracles.

The Egyptian god Osiris left me with this message after I met with him in a shamanic journey: "It doesn't take real strength when one uses only will. Real strength is when one can open and surrender to the powers that be."

In *Seedtime and Harvest* Neville inspires us to keep searching when he writes: "Transformation is in principle always possible, for the transformed being lives in us, and it is only a question of becoming conscious of it."[1]

In working with miracles, you must constantly work on the attitudes and rational beliefs you hold. These can prevent you from having the belief and faith not only that miracles occur, but that they can occur in your own life, too.

When you perceive that your work with transmutation has failed, look at what lesson you are missing. Look at what has changed by doing the work versus what your expectations were. Explore the lessons and opportunity for growth and change you are being presented with.

Let's not forget to acknowledge the issue of right timing. When your efforts to create change fail, look at whether you are pushing the river. Ask yourself: Do your life and your environment support the work you are trying to do right now?

When the fires were burning out of control in New Mexico, I performed a ceremony to ask the winds to calm down and the fire to abate. Even though the weather forecast predicted no chance of rain, I asked that rain come to bring some relief to the land. I asked for all of this if it was for the highest good of all concerned. I had tried to journey on why, from a spiritual perspective, this great catastrophe was occurring. I did not receive an answer. This is generally true when

I journey on "why" questions, as sometimes it is not time for us to understand the mysteries of the universe.

Although Santa Fe was not within danger of the fire, I asked that the land here be protected. As I have a great love for trees, I tend to direct my prayers to ask for help on behalf of the trees.

What I was told by my helping spirits was that although I thought my efforts to stop the wind and the fire and to bring rain had failed, my prayers to protect the trees in Santa Fe were being heard. I was directed to keep praying for the trees throughout the summer, when the fire danger would be great.

I kept up my prayers for the land and the trees. The fire began to approach sacred ruins on the Santa Clara Pueblo. I know many people's prayers went out into the spirit realms to stop destruction of these sites.

As the fire got close to the pueblo, a severe wind advisory for New Mexico went into effect. Although the rest of the state experienced very high winds, cloud cover prevented the winds from blowing in the area of the fire. When the winds did come the next day, they shifted to a different direction than expected, leading the fire backward over land that was already burned. This was a lesson that reminded me that help comes in ways that are not always expected.

Sometimes it is difficult for us as humans to know when our spiritual work is what we would call successful. But the spirits are listening and will respond when destiny can be redirected. What is important is to keep up the work.

Paracelsus believed that faith cures all ills, but few of us have the faith required to call forth a miracle.

Most of all, don't give up. We live in a world that desires instant enlightenment and fast-food spirituality. As I wrote in the Introduction, there is no shortcut to the path of spiritual enlightenment. You have to do your work; you must live your spiritual beliefs and ethics; and you must become and embody divine consciousness. This takes time and commitment to your spiritual path. Set your intention to love yourself and the spirit that lives in all things, to find harmony inside yourself, to be in union with the divine source of all life, to focus on and concentrate your efforts to embody your divinity, to use your imagination to envision a world that is free of darkness and in which all things are possible, and you will find that transmutation takes place in the way that embraces right timing and honors your own fate and destiny.

If you have changed at all from doing the work, you have not failed. The point of the work is not what you do in the world, but who you become. You cannot fail.

VI

Ceremonies for Transmutation

Imagine it's nighttime, and you're standing in a circle of friends. The black sky is lit up by the bright silver sliver of the new moon and the countless number of stars shining their brilliant light on you, reminding you of your own shine.

You are surrounded by your favorite trees, and a fire is burning and crackling in the middle of the circle. You can hear the nature spirits calling your name. The air is still, and you stand in awe of the beauty of the moment and in deep appreciation for the friends and nature around you.

An elder steps forward. She begins to shake a rattle and whistles, calling in and calling down the great loving spirit of all life. The hairs begin to stand up on your arms and the back of your neck as you feel the loving presence arrive. You are struck by the magic of this moment. The elder asks that the spirit of this place—the spirit of the earth, moon, sun, stars, rocks, trees, water, air, fire, insects, plants, and animals—be witness to the work about to be done tonight as each person present steps forth to fully express his soul. The elder reminds the group that it is everyone's birthright to fully express his soul, and she calls forth each person's divinity.

A breeze comes up, acknowledging that the spirits are here and listening. You feel the power of this place surge up your body, filling you with a rich fullness of energy.

The group begins to raise their voices in songs that come from the heart. An opening to the invisible worlds is created, and the miracle of healing and creation can now begin as each member opens his heart to the others, the spirit that lives in all things, and the creator.

It is your turn to step forward and state in loud, clear words your request to be blessed with a life filled with healing, abundance, wholeness, and harmony. After you call out your desire, you step up to the fire to place into it a talisman you have made. It is a stick of wood bound with plants and grasses you've used to weave in the beliefs and attitudes that block you from receiving and using the gifts of your divinity. You say good-bye to the limiting thoughts and realize that in a strange way they have become your friends, as you have heard those words for so many years.

You finally throw the empowered talisman in the fire. The group cheers as they love and support you in an unconditional way, knowing that as you heal, each of them heals. The spirits and the group receive you and hold you from a place of love. You feed the fire, the great transmuter, some dried cedar in thanks for transmuting your negative energy into healing energy.

You walk away from the fire and walk up to your favorite tree, where you leave an offering of your favorite flowers, a lock of hair, and your favorite sweet, and give thanks for your life.

20

The Nature of
Ceremonies

*[Ceremony] is the binding agent of culture and articulates
for man—through man—his place in nature and the
nature of his place, so that there is harmonious reciprocity
between the culture and its environment, making of the two
a seamless whole.*

—JOSÉ AND MIRIAM ARGÜELLES

Ceremonies and rituals are performed to honor the spirits; to honor and celebrate life and changes in nature; to honor, celebrate, and acknowledge rites of passage as used in initiations; to give thanks after the harvesting of crops; and to create change. Performing a ceremony or ritual will create transformation.

In my life and work I use the words *ceremony* and *ritual* interchangeably. As I began writing this chapter I pondered how and if the two are different for me. I thought about what situations I use the two words in. As I remembered past workshops and watched myself teaching groups, I discovered that I usually use *ritual* to imply healing work that will be repeated again and again over time. A ritual for healing might be repeated every day, once a week, or once a month. I tend to use the word *ceremony* when I talk about work the group will do once for healing and honoring ourselves or nature. The ceremony might be repeated again at a later time, but usually for a different issue.

In *Ritual, Power, Healing, and Community* Malidoma Somé, an African shaman, discusses how he sees the difference between ceremony and ritual. He says that in ritual it is our role to call to the spiritual world to intervene in our lives. We have to take the initiative to start the process, but then must let go of the results to the will of the forces we have called in. Somé says that we are only instruments in the interaction between dimensions and realms. He says, "There is a ritual each time a spirit is called to intervene in spiritual affairs. The structure of the ritual is what I would like to call ceremony because it can vary from time to time and from place to place. So ceremony, perhaps, is the anatomy of a ritual. It shows what actually is taking place in the visible world, on the surface, and can therefore be seen, observed, corrected."[1]

I find that people in our culture are afraid of performing ceremonies and rituals. Creating personal ceremonies and ritual is not part of our culture, and we are not taught about their power or how and why they are created. Ceremony and ritual remain mysterious to us, and things we don't understand we tend to fear. Or they may be associated with religious oppression.

Ceremonies and rituals are used to honor, celebrate, heal, and transmute. In performing ceremony and ritual we take an active role in creating our lives. Malidoma Somé says that "ritual links humans to the gods or God."[2] Jean Houston comments that in ancient Egypt, "The magus knows that anything set into motion—a work, an idea, a thought, a ritual—sends resonant waves throughout the whole system, changing everything."[3] Ceremony creates a relationship between the creator and your own divinity in such a way that allows you to become the sculptor of your life and world.

In cultures that still perform ceremonies that have been passed down through generations, the form is important. These ceremonies have been used with great intent, sometimes for centuries. As we no longer have healing ceremonies we can call our own, we must once again learn the ancient art of using ceremony and ritual for transmutation. It is not appropriate for us to use ceremonies that belong to other cultures, so we must create and perform personal ceremony or ritual. There is no right or wrong way to do this. There is, however, no power in performing a ceremony as if it were a recipe. The ceremony must have meaning to you personally if there is to be enough power created for successful results.

The form of the ceremony is not as important as making sure the essential elements are present. All ceremonies have a beginning, middle, and end. The beginning involves getting clear on the intention for the ceremony, the preparation, and the calling in of spiritual help. The middle is performing the ceremony itself. The end is thanking and releasing the spirits that have been called in to help. Let's use the formula for transmutation to provide us with the key elements needed.

First you must know your intention for wanting to perform the ceremony. Is this a ceremony of giving thanks? Are you wanting to honor a cycle in your life or nature? Is this a ceremony for asking for healing for yourself and/or the earth? Are you trying to call something into your life? It is important to work very carefully with intent. Ceremony and ritual do create change, and you must be careful about what you are calling into your life. Caroline Casey writes, "Neuroscientists have found that brain cells fire not just upon action, but immediately upon formation of an intention."[4]

You want to make sure that you are using ceremony and ritual to create harmony and work in partnership with the power of the universe. You don't want to use ceremony or ritual to manipulate the universe. I often observe rituals that look like a child's presenting his parents with a list of gifts he wants for Christmas. The child is not really thinking about whether these toys will ultimately bring happiness or whether he will still want the toys when they finally arrive.

Don't present the universe with a wish list without careful consideration of consequences. Make sure you are not creating your intent from an egoic state of "I want" or "give me." Do not beg the universe, but rather call down blessings to be bestowed on you. Use the methods you have learned to get into a deep meditative state where you can access the depth of what your soul is calling in and what your own spirit or divinity will support. Carefully consider whether you will want to receive what you are asking for at some future time. Consider whether you are asking for too much, which will cause you to feel overwhelmed when the universe answers your call. If you are unsure of the outcome you wish to receive, you might decide to ask for "Thy will be done."

Once you have stated your intent, you will need to concentrate on holding that intent during the ceremony or ritual. Focus is needed to create good results. If you begin to scatter your attention, you will lose the intent as well as the power.

When you know your purpose for performing a ceremony, you must now use your imagination to develop the form. Before addressing this step, let's consider the space you will need to create, which includes the state of consciousness you will need to attain.

It is crucial that you perform your ritual or ceremony in a state of harmony. You do not want to perform it in an emotionally charged state. Before performing rituals, we prepare to move into a state of personal harmony, thereby creating harmony with the power of the universe. This creates an opening that allows the spirits or the absolute to work through. To create harmony, the key is moving your ego out of the way so that the power of the universe can come in. As I wrote in Part I, song and dance were traditionally used to move oneself out of an egoic, separate state and into a state of connection and union. Experiment with using singing and dancing as a way to open, moving into partnership and union with the universe and out of an egoic, manipulative state. You can sing a song you have learned from others that opens your heart. You might try humming and allowing this to turn into a song. You might work on developing a special song that you sing only before you perform a ceremony. Experiment with movements that open your body, allowing you to breathe deeply. This will open your heart, providing the harmony and alignment with the spiritual forces needed to open the veils between the worlds where healing and creation can occur.

After coming up with your intent and preparing your state of being, the next step will be to call in the forces you are asking for help. Are you asking for help from the creator you have been working with, or are you calling in specific spirits, such as gods and goddesses or other guardian spirits? Be precise about whom you are calling in. This requires the elements of intention, focus, and concentration. You must come up with a way to call in and call down helping spiritual forces, as well as call forth your own divinity. Shamans use rattling, drumming, whistling, singing, and dancing. Remember that the keys to calling in are intent and having an open heart; you must make the form of doing this your own.

By following the above steps, using focus and concentration to hold your intention, you should now be in a state of harmony, love, and union. This is the state necessary before miracles can happen.

Before you do the preparation to change your state of consciousness, you will want to use your imagination to develop the actual ceremony. Think about how you are going call down the help you need. There might be some words you will want to say out loud, or you might want to use song and dance. You might want to create a ritual object to either leave on the earth or release to the elements. When you are done, thank the spirits you have called in to help, support, and witness the work and let them know the work is done.

The following includes some of the ceremonies I have created for different purposes. The suggestions given will come out of the material that you have already read in previous chapters. Some ceremonies you might wish to perform alone, and some will be more appropriate to perform in a group. These are just ideas that you can use to stimulate your imagination to create ceremonies that have meaning for you. Remember, the form is not as important as the sacred space you create. Make sure that you focus and concentrate on your intention and that you are in a state of harmony, love, and union with the rest of life before you begin your work. Other key ingredients to consider are: making sure you honor the spirits you have called in; honoring yourself; being certain you do not use power to manipulate others or the universe; being humble; respecting yourself and others; working in partnership with nature and the spirit that lives in all things; being thankful for your life as well as for the visible and invisible forms of life around you; and being grateful for all you have and all you have received.

The purpose of the ceremony is to invoke the spirits to ask them to provide some sort of help for you. The key, therefore, is creating a space where the lines of communication between you and the spirits are clear and where the spirits can come through to do the necessary work.

21

Ceremonies for Releasing

Fire is called the great transmuter by all spiritual traditions. As I was doing research for this book, all the definitions for the creator that I read about from various spiritual traditions included light or fire. Earlier in this book I said that the key for transmutation is understanding that all life is of the light, that you are light, that everything can be turned into light. So it does not surprise me that fire is seen as such a transformative force, since whatever you place in the fire is transmuted into light and goes back to the creator. Fire ceremonies have been performed for healing all over the world for thousands of years.

There are many forms that you can use for fire ceremonies. You can work in a group where each person has the opportunity to do releasing work with the power of the community for support. When I lead workshops in which we perform a fire ceremony, the key elements of the power of the healing are the fire and the support of the circle.

The ceremony can be very simple or can take more commitment and work on your part. You must decide if putting more work into the ceremony will create more healing for you. You can simply burn a piece of paper containing words describing what you are releasing to the fire. You can spend a day or days making a talisman empowered with what you are releasing. There's a teaching from shamanism we can use here: Shamanic art does not represent power; shamanic art *is* power. In making a talisman or object, the talisman needs to be empowered with what you are releasing; it is not a representation. First you want to decide on materials that you can use; they must be things that are natural and will burn. You want to make your object in silence, so that you can release what is in you into the object itself. Some ways you might want to empower this talisman is to sing in, talk in, rattle in, drum in, or dance in what you are releasing. Do not share what you are releasing until you have completed your ceremony, as talking disperses and breaks the power.

Before you do the actual ceremony of releasing, make sure you are ready to say good-bye to what you are letting go of. You can dance what you are releasing, you can sing, you can rattle or drum, or you can state out loud what you are letting go of. If you are working with a group, chanting, drumming, or rattling throughout the ceremony will help the group maintain its power and focus. Use all the elements discussed in working with ceremony, but make sure you thank the fire for the healing. I give cedar to the fire in thanks. You can give a dried plant of any kind that feels like an offering from your heart, or a favorite food. Recognize and acknowledge that you are not dumping negativity into nature; instead, you are transmuting the energy into light. Thank the spirits you have called in, and state that the work is done.

Ceremonies for releasing can include:

* Negative and false beliefs and attitudes you have identified that block you from using your creative potential and owning your divinity.
* Negative feelings that you hold about someone else. By releasing these feelings back to the light, you are now released from this person.
* Negative thoughts and sabotaging beliefs that keep looping in

your mind and hold you back from falling into the arms of the loving universe and living life as the adventure it was intended to be.

* Negative thoughts or beliefs that prevent you from receiving nurturance from yourself, food, people, and the creator.
* Beliefs about why you can't make the changes in your life that will move you to a place of healing, abundance, and harmony.
* Fears that prevent you from living fully.
* Anything that weighs you down, preventing you from connecting with the spiritual forces in you and around you.
* Anything that prevents you from receiving the energy of light and life and giving it back in your role of caretaker of the earth.

In keeping with the principle that light is the transmuting force, you could do a visualization of releasing to the light associated with your creator.

22

Ceremonies for Calling Down

Just as you can perform a ceremony or ritual to release something that is blocking your journey through life, you can call down support that will be helpful to you. Once again I must stress ethics. Please do not use rituals to call down desires that come from the ego instead of divine spirit. If you move your life into a place of harmony, you will be able to manifest those things that fill you up. You might work to call down health, meaningful work, meaningful relationships (friends, community, or a life partner), help in expressing your creativity, or help in being a caretaker of the earth. Think about and journey or meditate on what your true heart's desire might be. Give this careful consideration.

Using the magical power of sound, come up with words you want to state out loud, or again, you can make a talisman of natural materials that you empower with your heart's desire and leave in a power spot. You can visualize putting your heart's desire in a balloon and seeing it flying high into the ether, carrying your message of what you are asking for. Use your imagination to create a ritual that will call down help and send a message for what you need right now in your life to feel fulfilled.

Once you have prepared yourself and your space, if you are in harmony and union with the divine, your prayer will be heard. The universe will bring to you what you have asked for, but not always in the form you expect. As long as you ask for what is in service of your highest good and "Thy will be done," you will find that you get what your soul has called in.

As I have written earlier, you can use ceremony to retrieve the soul of a piece of land, a house, or an office. Everything that is alive has a soul, an essence, a life force that might have been lost or never called in. I think it is a bit presumptuous to call in the soul of the earth; if the consciousness of people has not changed, how will this soul be cared for? Start smaller.

There might be a piece of land that you know of and like to visit, or maybe the land you live on, that feels devoid of life force. If you have been working on healing your own soul and becoming more present in life, the lack of life force in a place will become obvious to you. We must not project that land has been traumatized because of a fire, hurricane, earthquake, or other disaster; in fact, usually the land is healed in some way by these forces. For example, fires create the heat needed to allow certain seeds to germinate, and wind and rains often have a cleansing effect. People are traumatized by natural occurrences such as these, but the land is usually fine. You must tune in and let go of your human projections for a moment to ask whether or not this land is missing essence. Trust the truth you feel in your bones.

There are endless ceremonies you can use to call in the soul of a place, so be creative. Singing back the soul, rattling, and bringing offerings of food, flowers, or healing herbs will all work to entice the soul back to the land. You must use your intention, focus, concentration, and love to reach out to the soul and call it back in. Working in a group definitely is best. First, this way of working creates more power for the healing, as all those in the group open their hearts with one intention; also, it changes the consciousness of people involved. Each person will now know and understand that land, the earth, has a soul. Once consciousness has been changed, we change how we

treat the places where we live, therefore supporting the life force of the land we live on, creating a healing environment to live in.

The same work can be done with a house or office. Today the art of building spaces has been lost. Often we find that contractors are told to build as fast and as cheaply as they can. There was a time when great thought and care went into the materials and design, when love and power went into the process of building. Building was considered a work of art. We still see this today in some cases, but it is not the norm. The result is that many of us live and work in soulless places. This has an effect on our emotional and physical health, as our own soulfulness is not being mirrored back to us. Our souls crave living and working in spaces filled with energy and life force. We have all had the experience of walking into a building where one can breathe and relax into how good it feels to be there, where something just feels right.

Healing and calling in the soul to structures is possible and can be easily done. In houses I use singing, rattling, and placing special objects in each room to accomplish this task. I also put my attention to physically cleaning every inch of the house with love to call in the soul. In an office, I try to advise people to work simply, especially if coworkers might be put off by behaviors unfamiliar to them. Bringing in artwork, fresh flowers, or other things from nature (rocks, shells, pieces of wood) with intention, concentration, and love will call down the soul.

You can also perform a ceremony to call blessings down into your life. Again the key is to state a clear intention to the spirits; only then can you design a ritual. Recently I was leading a ceremony marking the beginning of the new year. I placed a bowl of water in the middle of the room and asked that the spirits come down and bless the water so that all who drank of it would receive blessings for the coming year.

In this particular ritual, the spirits let us know without a doubt that they were coming in. As I called in the spirits with a rattle the wind began to howl and was so strong that the building we were in rocked. We used singing and toning to transfigure into the divine forces who would bless this water. As we toned, what was at first a drizzle outside turned into an incredible downpour. It was strong enough that I wondered if we were going to wash away. When we finished, the rain began to lessen and the wind stopped blowing.

To end the ceremony, I had people use the power of words to send up a prayer for themselves and the planet. A great deal of time went by, and people were still coming up with more things to ask for. I wasn't sure how to say, "Okay, that's enough for now." Again the spirits came into play. An intense rain began once again, this time creating so much noise as it hit the building that we could no longer hear each other. The message was received by our group and the work was done. The next day the sun was shining brightly and there was not a cloud in the sky.

Everyone in the room was so struck how nature responded to each part of the ceremony to let us know the presence of the spirits we called in.

Ceremonies for Working in Partnership

Miracles happen when we work in a creative partnership with the natural world, as I have mentioned earlier. Findhorn and Perelandra are examples of the extraordinary plants and vegetables that can be produced when working in partnership with the nature spirits.

People around the world have also been able to work with the weather spirits in a creative partnership. There are many tales of shamans being able to bring rain to drought-afflicted areas or bring sun to places drenched with flooding rains.

Ethics are once again important in doing this kind of work. You must consider why you want to work with the weather. Consider whether you want a weather change for a trivial reason, such as you don't want a picnic rained out. If so, is this for the highest good of all life in this area? The key here is to ask for the highest good of all life, not just for you. You don't want to use spiritual methods to manipulate the powers that be. You want to use spiritual methods to be in a place of power *with* the forces of nature, not *over* the forces of nature. As a caretaker of the earth, you must use this ability for the good of all.

In the late 1990s Santa Fe experienced the worst drought in over a hundred years. Many groups had gathered to perform ceremonies to bring rain. I worked on my own. I did my usual ceremonies, as well as painted a picture to draw down and entice the rain to Santa Fe. After I painted the picture, I noticed a few raindrops. I decided to journey to the spirits and ask why the ceremonies performed were not successful. The reply I received was that people living in Santa Fe had forgotten they were living in a desert and were not honoring the land. At this time people were flocking to live in Santa Fe, and the growth that was occurring was quite scary to those already living there. The drought brought an end to new building permits, and people started to realize that living in a desert required the conservation of water. The drought proved effective in bringing people back into some sense of harmony and balance with the land. Since the drought ended, building permits are now being given out with more thought to water conservation.

It's also important not to take credit if you are successful in working with weather. When we move into a place of self-importance, saying, "Look at what I did," we forget that we are just one small piece of the puzzle. When we brag about our power, we lose it. That seems to be one of those laws of the universe that keeps harmony and balance.

To avoid letting one's ego get blown out of proportion, you might consider working with a group when doing a ceremony to affect the weather. In this way, no one person can take credit for any successes. When I work with the weather, I try to choose times when it will be difficult to determine my influence on the outcome. In Santa Fe, the weather work I perform usually involves trying to call down moisture. I pick my time to work when the clouds are thick and there is a possibility of rain. This brings in the principle of ambiguity, where one is left in the dark as to what forces are really at work. This of course doesn't lend itself to scientific proof, but it works well to help us remain open to the mysteries of how things work in the universe.

Going with the principle that all life has a spirit, one can work with the spirit in the elements that create weather changes. When the forest fires were out of control in Brazil, the Yanomani Indians called in the wind to blow the smoke away and then called in the rain.

The Yanomani, accustomed to the humid depths of a green forest, were terrified. "We couldn't see the fire, only the smoke," Davi Yanomani recalled. "We couldn't see the sun. We couldn't hunt. We were surrounded. We were afraid."

Since they had never seen such smoke, the tribe members had no special ceremony to make the fire go away. So they improvised. They used rituals usually performed to heal the sick. And they accepted the help of Kaiapo shamans from Xingu, a region in the central Amazon, transported to Roraima by a government willing to try anything.

In the waning days of March, the shamans gathered. First, they sniffed the hallucinogenic bark of the virola tree, which sent them into a trance. They sang and danced in rituals that they believed would help them communicate with the spirits of the universe.

The first ritual they improvised was designed to ask for wind, to blow the smoke away. The second, to stop the fire. The third, to bring rain to Demini.

Then the shamans repeated the rituals for the people on other parts of Roraima state. "We sent the spirits of rain to Apiau, and to Catrimani," he said.

On March 29, the shamans performed another ceremony. This was to clear the air and provide a safe plane trip for Davi Yanomani, who was preparing to go to far-off Brasilia to speak to the government about the effect of the fires on his people.

Late March 30, and in the early hours of March 31, the rains began to fall over much of Roraima.[1]

In this particular case the shamans appealed to the spirit of the elements. I, too, have worked with appealing to and calling in the weather spirits themselves. For me, the first step is to take my rattles and go outside and begin rattling and singing a power song, which brings me into connection with the universal power. I sing for a long time, until I notice an opening between the worlds. This feeling that an opening has occurred is obvious to me on an intuitive level. My perception shifts, and there is no longer a separation between me and the spirit world. As I move into a state of harmony I perceive the world around me in harmony.

Once this shift happens, I change the song I sing. Inspired in the moment, I sing words that appeal to the weather spirits to help bring the rain that will feed the plants, the trees, the rocks, the insects, the birds, the animals, and the earth, all of which need the nurturance of water to survive. I send my decree loudly through the air to ask for help on behalf of all of life. I use singing and dance movements to call down the rain. I don't beg; I ask for the help needed. I ask for harmony and balance to be restored to the land again. I let go of the results, knowing that if I ask for what is best for all of life to survive, my call will be answered—sometimes in unexpected ways.

When I am through I leave an offering to the weather spirits, thanking them for listening to my request. I like to leave blue corn-meal as an offering when I perform rituals. Blue is my favorite color, and corn is a very sacred food for me. This offering has great meaning for me, as I truly believe that I am leaving a sacred gift. I love chocolate, so I usually leave some chocolate, too. Both of these are used in numerous indigenous cultures. There are other offerings I may leave, depending on what my heart feels the spirits would like or what the spirits themselves indicate.

When I do this ceremony, I do it in the same place and in the same way. Over the years of working in this manner, I keep feeling more power and ease in communication with the spirits I am calling in.

Sometimes when I teach workshops in places where the weather is extreme, I have found honoring and thanking the ancestors of the place an effective way to produce weather changes. In places where there are flooding rains, after I speak to the ancestor spirits the rain has stopped and the sun comes out. After speaking to the ancestors where there is a drought, sometimes it rains.

As you learn to connect and communicate with the spirit of the place where you live as well as the nature spirits, you will find that there are many helping spirits that you can call on to assist as you ask for harmony to be restored. For example, during a journey, the spirits told me that when one lives in a mountainous area, it is the mountains that create weather. I was instructed to connect with the spirit of the mountain in Santa Fe as I prayed for rain. You might find that one way to affect changes in weather is through your connection with the earth itself.

I want to remind you of the story I retold in Part IV, in which a man known for his weather work was called in to bring rain to a drought-ridden area. The man had seen that the problem was that the village was out of balance and order. He asked to spend some time away from the people of the village. Once he found harmony in himself, he returned, and it began to rain. The teaching in this story is that when you are in harmony, the environment you live in will reflect back that harmony. Harmony is such an important key to transmutation.

PARTNERSHIP WITH HEALTH CARE PROFESSIONALS

So far I have been teaching you to use spiritual methods to work with toxins in the body and in the environment—to create harmony. In all spiritual traditions, doctors and healers have worked in partnership. In dealing with illness we need to address body, mind, and spirit. I find often that when people seek help from the medical profession, there is an imbalance of power. People don't see themselves as working in partnership with doctors for their own health and well-being. I often hear words like these reported by patients: "They are going to do this to me," "I don't understand a word the doctor said, but this is what he told me he is going to do," "I don't feel good about the treatment planned for me, but I guess I will go along with it." Statements such as these don't lend themselves to true healing. I instruct clients that when you go to a doctor or into surgery, you must see that you are working in partnership with your doctor to get well. If you don't understand the treatment planned, ask more questions so that you feel you are part of the planning. Learn to distinguish the difference between egoic fear and intuition. If your intuition says the treatment is wrong, communicate this to your doctor.

The key here is to change the words you use and the attitude that something is being done to you. Begin to use language that implies there is a creative partnership between you and your health care professionals for your healing. Before going to see a doctor or other health care professional, form a strong intention that you are invoking the power of creative partnership. Before going into surgery, call in the power of your creator or the helping spirits you work with as well as your own soul to lend help and support to the physical procedure.

24

Ceremonies for Transformation and Healing

The key I have been emphasizing in this chapter on ceremonies is that creating a state of harmony will affect the results of the ceremony you perform. Your inner state will affect your outer state, thereby having an impact on the results of your transmutation work. I also must stress the power of love in performing ceremonies for transmutation. Love heals. You can learn endless techniques and ceremonies for healing, but if love is not present, there will be no power. Techniques do not heal; love does. To help you prepare for your ceremony and place you into a state of harmony and love, you can use any of the exercises in Part II as well as the dismemberment exercise in Part V. Remember, singing or toning will always open your heart and connect you with the power of the universe. We have also seen how spiritual masters have used transfiguration, changing from the human egoic self to a being of divine light, then using this power of light to heal and transmute.

Any ceremony for transmutation must be created with light and love. Of course, the other ingredients—intention, harmony, union, focus, concentration, and imagination—need to be added also. By getting into a state of harmony and love, becoming in union with the divine, focusing on the intention to heal, keeping yourself concentrated on the work in hand, and using your imagination to envision successful results, you can create the energy needed for transmutation to occur.

HARMONIZING WITH THE UNIVERSE

Besides working with the exercises in other chapters, as I have suggested, you can work with the following visualization to prepare for your healing work, putting you in harmony with the universe. Get into a quiet, relaxed state. Close your eyes and take a few deep breaths. Allow your energy to go out as far as it can, reaching toward the horizon of the universe above you, below you, in front of you, and behind you. Reach your arms out and allow your energy to move to the ends of the universe. Your energy field is formless and knows no bounds. Experience the feeling of becoming unburdened by your earthly needs and concerns as you do this.

Now begin to breathe with the following intention:

Breathe in light. Breathe out light.
Breathe in love. Breathe out love.
Breathe in peace. Breathe out peace.
Breathe in the power of the universe. Breathe out the power of the universe.
Breathe in harmony. Breathe out harmony.

Continue to do this until you reach a state of consciousness in which you feel ready to do the ceremony you intend.

TRANSMUTATION OF NEGATIVE THOUGHTS

This ceremony works well for those days where you find yourself consumed with negative thoughts about yourself or others.

Light a candle and sit a few feet away from it. Send your negative thoughts to the light of the candle to be transmuted. Keep this up until you feel free from your obsessive thoughts.

Now let the light of the candle feed your body. In return, feed the fire of the candle with your love.

TRANSMUTING THE FOOD THAT NOURISHES YOU

The physical form of nurturance we need to survive is food. As I have described in Part IV, we don't place enough importance on what we choose to eat and how it is prepared. Cooking food must become a sacred ritual for true nurturance to take place. If you cook food from a place of anger or depression, there will be a toxic effect on your body. Creating sacred space for food preparation must become a part of your spiritual practice. Before you begin to do any food preparation, think about your ceremony. All food preparation is a ceremony, whether you are aware of it or not. If you perform your ceremony from a rushed or emotionally charged state, it will affect the energy that is put into the food. Think about the ceremony you are about to perform. Move into a place of love and compassion for the person or persons you are preparing the food for, even if it is just for yourself. If you can simply change your consciousness when you prepare your food, you will be amazed at how much the energy of the food changes.

If you know that you are using ingredients that have not been harvested or slaughtered from a place of love and honor, call the divine into the food. Use the power of intention to do this. Embody your creator to bring divine love and light into the food. Once you attain a state of union, you can pray over your food, or you can also try bringing light and love to the food by holding your hands over it. Chant over your food. Call down blessings into your food using words of power. If you are not nurtured from what you eat, how can you be a source of love? Food must be a source of nutrition and love for you to thrive and create a good world. Always give thanks for the life sacrificed so that you might live.

Through the earth, the creator brings us the food that will nurture us. When we do not receive the offering and gifts from the creator, we dishonor the divine source of all life, implying that we reject life. Food collects light from the heavens and nourishment from the earth. To honor the divine and life itself, you must honor and appreciate the gifts you are receiving as you eat and nourish yourself. Concentrating on the principle of honoring the source of this food and giving thanks as you eat will naturally transmute your food into a source of healing. When I eat, I like to repeat silently to myself these words: "All life is of the light, I am light, this food is light, I gratefully receive this light into my body to nourish and heal me." It sounds like a lot of words, but when you become used to this thinking, they are quite comforting. Once again you can place your hands over your food with the intention of bringing through the light of the divine before you eat.

TRANSMUTING THE ENERGY OF A SPACE

We can also look at using ceremony to release or clear negative energies in a room. Here again, the form is not important. What is important is to remember that being in a state of harmony and love will change your external world.

Your imagination and your own creative genius will help you develop ways to clear a space. I tend to take things literally sometimes, and when I feel a space needs cleansing, I literally clean. I vacuum. As I clean I hold the intention of asking for the power of love and light to return to this space, and it does. I have never been in a place I have not been able to clear of negative energy and thought forms.

Some traditions use different kinds of incense to clear a room. The Native Americans use sage, cedar, or sweetgrass, the Australian natives use eucalyptus leaves, and some shamans in South America use copal. I suggest burning herbs or incense that is pleasing to you. If a smell is pleasing to you, your own healing and divine energy will infuse the space you are in.

Simply through intention and concentration, ask that the light of the divine or your creator come and fill the space with divine love. This works especially well if you are in a room with people who are putting out negative emotions. As long as you are in union with the divine, there will be no opening inside yourself for this energy to enter. Through intention you can ask to merge with and be filled with the power of your creator, which will provide you with any protection you might need. Allow your own luminescence to come forth to light up the room you are in.

TRANSMUTING BY PERCEIVING ALL ENERGY AS NEUTRAL

Another way to work with negative energy is to simply understand that all energy is just energy and can be perceived as neutral. Many years ago I was teaching a workshop on shamanism. One night after class I taught the group a game involving the art of shamanic seeing in the visible world. The game is called the bone game, and it is played in teams. Basically, two people on one team hide bones in their clasped hands. One bone in each hand is blank and one has a line on it. A person on the other team must "see" the marked bone in the hiders' hands. One of the tasks of the hiders' team is to try to break the concentration of the person trying to "see" by making loud noises and distracting movements.

In teaching this game, every few years I find someone very gifted in the art of "seeing." When this occurs, I ask the person how he or she works, for I know he or she is using a strategy. In this particular workshop, there was one woman who seemed to be unusually gifted. After speaking with her, I was impressed by her perception of energy. She is a professional cello player. When she performs in concert, the audience puts out a great deal of energy. Some people are excited and pleased, while some might be tired or bored. Some people might be dealing with the angers and disappointments of their day, while some might be content. This woman sees all energy as neutral energy. Whether a person sitting in the room is angry, happy, content, or bored, he or she is just putting out energy. She perceives all this energy as neutral energy, which she uses to help her perform. In the bone game, she used all the distracting energy put out by the hiding team to give her the energy to see.

Thus energy is just energy. Once it has been created, it cannot be destroyed. We live on a planet of duality. This principle of duality is what creates the judgment that some energy is bad while some is good. When you move into a divine space, there is no duality, just union. Therefore there is no positive or negative. We can use this principle to transmute any energy that feels negative by experiencing it as pure energy that can be used.

Just imagine walking down a crowded city street where the air is thick with strong emotions, some positive, others negative, and perceiving them as neutral energy that could empower you in your day. This is the true meaning of transmutation. If one person can do it, so can you. Until we learn how to fill our environment with love, we must use our intention and concentration to transmute the energy that does exist into either neutral or loving energy.

THE TRANSMUTATION OF WATER

As I work with water, I hold the intention not just to transmute the pollution in the water, but to transmute it into holy water that can nourish and heal anyone who drinks or touches it. When I have journeyed for advice on this work, I keep receiving the same message: "Water, by its nature, reflects back your own soul. To create pure and holy water, you must become pure and holy." Before you attempt to transmute water, you must do the preparation required to place you into the state you wish to have reflected back to you.

I suggest working with the element of water because it tends to be the easiest element to transmute. I had a student in the early 1980s who lectured on paranormal phenomena. He shared with the group I was teaching that the nature of water changes when it is present at a healing. There are reports of successful experiments transmuting water with crystals charged with a healing intention, as well as transmutation occurring through special chants.

There are Vedic as well as Sufi chants designed for transmutation. These chants are ancient and have been handed down by serious students of these systems for hundreds of years. As we no longer have chants of our own, we have to develop new ones. Remember what the ancient Hindus and Egyptians knew about the magical properties of sound and words. Our state of consciousness added to the power of sound and the use of words can create transmutation.

Meditate or journey on sounds and words that you can develop into a chant for transmutation. Go to the spiritual helpers you work with or the divine power you have learned to communicate with. Students of many traditions have found that toning beginning with the syllable *aum* can be quite healing.

As you chant or tone, you will notice that your energy expands and that your state of consciousness has changed. You are now an empty vessel, or what in shamanism is called the "hollow bone," creating the space for the power of the divine forces you work with to come through. I find that toning facilitates the process of transfiguration into the divine.

Bless the water with your words. Move your hands over the container of water and allow the light coming through you to infuse the water with light. Merge with the water, letting it reflect your state of purity and love while calling forth the water's own divine nature. Using all your senses, imagine the water to be pure and holy. Visualize it as pure, feel it as pure, touch its purity, and smell and taste its purity. I have found that merging with the water you are working with to be a secret to the success of this work.

One of the keys is to get into a state of union with the one heartbeat. You want to create a space where you ask and allow the water to change, instead of trying to make something happen.

You can work with regular drinking water to turn it into holy water. All water is holy water, but we have forgotten this, much as we have forgotten our own divinity. Taste the water before and after and notice any changes you perceive in how it tastes or how it feels to your body after you drink it.

If you choose to work with polluted water, you will need to test the water before and after your work. You might experiment with using chants or toning you have created for the purpose of transmutation versus just chanting or toning with no intention in mind. You might find that there is more power and faster results when working in a group rather than working alone. The spirits have advised me to work with water polluted by chemicals rather than polluted by living beings such as bacteria, since they also have a right to the water.

This is "big work." It will take time, patience, faith, and experimentation to see results. Don't give up after one try. Think of how long you have lived in a world of pollution, and allow yourself the time needed to fully learn the spiritual practices required to reverse this. And don't forget one of the most powerful keys, which is to imagine the possibility that you can be successful.

See the Epilogue for how a group I led worked with this ceremony and what we learned from it.

25

Ceremonies for Celebration and Honoring

People have always celebrated nature's changes. As we celebrate the changes inherent in the lunar and solar cycles, we create a vibrant connection between ourselves and the natural world. Dances are performed by members of communities and feasts are prepared. Among the Druid and pagan traditions there are very formal ceremonies, including certain invocations to the forces of nature, as well as songs sung and poems read out loud.

In developing your own ceremony, you must choose the elements you wish to honor and celebrate. Working in a group on celebrating changes in the moon and seasons establishes a conscious connection not just to nature, but to the community you live in. Sharing the preparation of food and eating together honors the changes in the moon and sun that nurture the growth of the food that sustains us. Giving our thanks through song and dance creates union and harmony with the forces in nature.

It is common for an outbreak of colds and flu to occur as a seasonal change begins. The body knows a change is coming, but the only way most people have to prepare for this change is to become ill, forcing them to slow down. Imagine if we intentionally chose to slow down and honor the change to come. Harmony would return to our body, mind, and spirit during these transitions, supporting our body and helping us stay healthy as the seasons turn.

Ceremony can also be used in this same way to honor life changes as we are initiated into new seasons and phases in our own life. Gather a group who will help you collect and maintain the energy and support you need to move with grace through the river of life.

Throughout our spiritual practice we call in divine energy. As we have already seen, some people work with one absolute power, while others might work with one divine source as well as intermediary spirits. Some people work with guardian angels, some with power animals, some with nature spirits, and some with different manifestations of the absolute through intermediary gods and goddesses.

Building a relationship through feeding and showing loyalty and commitment to the spirits you work with establishes a creative partnership between the visible and invisible forces, thereby creating a vortex, doorway, or opening for the spirits to come through.

Offering food and incense to your helping spirits is a way of honoring them. Giving thanks through your heart and thoughts each day as well as at special times keeps the partnership strong. Writing a poem about the spirit or spirits you call down for help, painting a picture of the divine, and dancing in honor of the gods and goddesses are all ways of giving thanks. In ancient Egypt some gave offerings of food and incense to the *neters* (the gods and goddesses). But most believe that the *neters* did not need material gifts; they just needed to know that they were honored in people's hearts. When you honor and nurture any relationship, that relationship will strengthen and will keep growing. As you feed your visible relationships, the same must be done with the invisible partners you call down into your life.

Every day of your life is filled with ceremony. Throughout the day you state your intention and call forth creations with your thoughts, emotions, and words. You have been living the life you have called forth and created. Up to this point, most of you have probably done this without consciousness of the process.

Imagine the possibilities now that you know how to sculpt your life and the health of the planet. Imagine!

To heal the earth through transmutation, you can use the power of ritual and ceremony to reestablish the connection with the divine forces needed to make healing successful. You can once again bring through divine energy to roam the earth while weaving the earthly and heavenly realms together.

Parts of the formula for transmutation used here:

Intention: In creating a ceremony, a strong intention is needed to let the divine or the helping spirits know what kind of help is being asked for. You must use intention to call in and call down the help needed.

Love: The greatest call for help to divine forces comes from the heart. Loving yourself and the community present at a ceremony creates an opening for healing and transmutation to occur.

Harmony: Before performing a ceremony or ritual, you must move yourself into a place of harmony with yourself and life by singing, dancing, or meditation.

Union: It is the union with the divine that creates transformation through ceremony.

Focus: You must focus on the purpose of your ceremony for the work to be successful.

Concentration: In order for power to be present and manifested during a ceremony, concentration is needed to hold the intention as well as hold the energy required to create sacred space. You must create sacred space for the divine to enter.

Imagination: You must be able to call upon your own imagination to put together a ceremony for a specific intention, as well as envision the work being successful.

Final Thoughts

W hen I was consulting with a water lab about possible tests for water pollution, the head of the lab had an interesting response to the ideas in this book. He asked, "Would the water change, or would the people performing the healing work change so that the contents of the water wouldn't be harmful to them?"

We want to use the material in this book to actually reverse environmental pollution. But it's also important to recognize that you will become a different person after doing the exercises, meditations, and ceremonies. It's not just what you do but who you become that will heal you and the earth.

After reading *Medicine for the Earth*, you might not be able to turn water into wine. But through the process of focusing on your intention, you will become more centered, grounded, and present, and so the quality of your life will improve.

In yogic terms, the goal of the yogi is to collect and gather *prana* (life force) within the body instead of the energy being dispersed. Through the exercises presented here, you have gathered and focused your energies to harmonize with the movement of life.

In addition to the formula of intention + love + harmony + union + focus + concentration + imagination = transmutation, some other keys to remember are:

The invisible worlds and helping spirits do exist. By learning to communicate with the beings in these realms we can develop a creative partnership, bringing the miracle of transmutation into a reality.

All the answers you are searching for will come through being still, not through activity.

Harmony within creates harmony without.

See the beauty in all things to open the veils between the worlds, to change your perception, and to experience that heaven is on earth now.

Know your divinity and shine your divine light, which reflects back the divine light in all life, especially the stars above us in the night sky.

May your harmonious prayers of beauty and love shower back down on you, all living things, and the earth.

Epilogue

On January 8 and 9, 2000, Diana, Gail, and Kate arrived at my house for our first weekend experiment with transmutation. They had been reading a draft of *Medicine for the Earth* as I was writing it and worked as a group with the material. Woods, my husband, who teaches yoga and meditation, joined us. We had been preparing for months to try to transmute water that had been polluted with chemicals. As I said in Part V, my helping spirits told me that transmuting water containing living beings was a complex issue and that I should focus on chemical pollution, which is responsible for so much illness.

When I shared this information with Troy at the Good Water Company, he suggested we work with water and gasoline, as the change in hydrocarbon content could be tested. Before our weekend I went to Good Water, where we made a control batch of 300 ml of water to 5 ml of gasoline. I took the rest of the gasoline and water I had brought to Good Water home to work with.

Diana's husband is a physicist, and Diana asked him if there was something we could use that would give us results as we worked. He made up a bottle of deionized water as well as a bottle of ammonium hydroxide for us. Deionized water is water that has no minerals or contaminants in it. Ammonium hydroxide comes from decaying vegetable matter and is a by-product of human or animal wastes. This is a very common contaminant that makes soil very alkaline and water undrinkable. It has a distinctive odor and a foul taste, so creatures will not drink it. It does have the capability to break down cell walls in the digestive tract, but the odds of someone drinking a concentration high enough to do this are low. The key here is that the water is no longer usable when the ammonium hydroxide is present.

Ammonium hydroxide makes fatty acids more soluble in water. This can make other pollutants such as petroleum products water soluble. This increases the danger of petroleum in the environment by enabling it to spread faster. Therefore ammonium hydroxide is a contaminant in itself and also harmful in terms of its effect on some other contaminants.

When placed in deionized water, the ammonium hydroxide makes the water very alkaline. We used pH test strips to test the deionized water and then the solution of ammonium hydroxide in water before we started. We also used pH test strips to test our results.

The other substance that we worked with was quinine. If you put quinine water (tonic water) in a dark mug and shine a light on it, you see that it is blue. Quinine is not harmful, but since we could see the color change as we worked, we used it also.

We spent Saturday and Sunday preparing for our evening ceremonies. Each night we used a different method. Saturday night we worked with divine intervention, asking the helping spirits and divine forces to transmute the water. Sunday night we worked with transfiguration into the divine, attempting to transmute the water.

Before each journey Woods led us in yoga postures and breathing exercises that helped oxygenate our bodies, which in turn woke us up and cleared our minds. We all agreed that this was a wonderful combination.

On Saturday the purpose of our first journey was to ask for advice on the appropriate ritual for divine intervention. The second journey was to merge with water, as I described in Part IV. The spirits emphasized the need to create a space for the divine to come through as well as the importance of our work as a community. We were told to make sure we were a strong circle filled with love that evening. This was very easy to accomplish, as we were a harmonious group.

We were also shown how water is a living being and that we were getting ready to kill it by adding the gasoline to it. This brought up many issues for members in the group. In her journey, Gail received that it was important for us to walk into the room one at a time and introduce ourselves to the water and establish a relationship with it. We also decided that before adding our contaminants to the water, we would use ceremony to create holy water, which would not be affected by the pollutants.

We spent the rest of the afternoon learning different chants that we wanted to use. Woods taught us a Vedic chant as well as some other Eastern chants. Diana taught us a Sufi chant that she works with in her spiritual practice.

We waited until it was dark to perform our ceremony. We were blessed with a beautiful new moon shining into the window as we began. The next step was to prepare our space. I put down a large scarf that I had used as an altar in the King's Chamber. On it we placed water we had gathered from sacred places around the earth. I had sacred water from Egypt, Tibet, and Turkey. Gail had water from Nepal. We lit five different candles and placed them around the room and burned some incense. We placed the water we were going to use in their respective glass containers. I carefully measured out 300 ml of the same water used in our control into a beaker. Diana placed the deionized water into a bowl. On this night we did not work with the quinine water. We brought in our drums and rattles and ceremonial objects we wanted present at our ceremony.

We all left the room and then filed in again. We held hands, and I shared some words that I felt would bind us as a circle to create a strong, loving community. I led the meditation of harmonizing with the forces of the universe, described in Part VI. Using my rattle and whistling, I called in our helping spirits, the helping spirits of the land, water, air, fire, and earth, stating our appreciation to them. We also honored the sun, moon, and stars. We all stated what we were asking the spirits for. On this night we focused on asking for the water to be healed. I reminded us of the seven parts of the transmutation formula that needed to be present for our work to be successful.

We continued creating our space and preparing for the work to be done by using our drums and rattles as we danced and sang our power songs. We sang the chants we had practiced that afternoon.

We then held our intention to make the water before us holy. We sang to the water. We all held the containers of water, asking for the spirit of the divine to enter this water and wake up its divinity.

When we felt we were done, Woods used kinesiology to test the water to see if it was ready to receive the pollutants. Applied kinesiology, used by some chiropractors, acupuncturists, and other alternative therapists, is a way to diagnose problems in the body. In this system, muscle testing is involved. There are many different forms of muscle testing. A common way is to have a client hold up an arm while holding a substance in question. If the substance is toxic to the body, when the practitioner pushes down on the arm it will fall dramatically. If the substance is beneficial, the arm will not fall when pushed on. Another way is for a person to put together the thumb and index finger while holding the substance or thinking about it. The ease with which you can pull the fingers apart indicates whether a substance is a problem or strengthens the body. You can perform muscle testing on yourself using the method involving pulling apart fingers.

Woods, an acupuncturist, is experienced at working with applied kinesiology. When he used his way of muscle testing, he reported that the field of energy on the water was expansive and that he felt that our work had been successful.

Diana tested the pH of the deionized water so that we had the starting point. The pH was 5.5. She then put in two droppers of ammonium hydroxide and again tested the water. The pH went up to 11.5, which is very alkaline and poisonous to drink. At the same time I measured 5 ml of gasoline and placed it into the other beaker of water. Woods used kinesiology once again and said that both waters tested as harmful to all the organs in the body. You can only imagine the fumes we were dealing with having so much gasoline in the water. This added to the urgency of our intention not only for our sake but as a reminder of the seriousness of worldwide water pollution.

We continued with singing our songs and calling in the helping spirits and divine forces to intervene in transmuting the water. Woods tested the water again and felt that we had not yet been successful. Diana tested the water with ammonium hydroxide using a pH test strip and found that the pH had gone down to 9, which is safe for drinking (at that point we did not know what a pH of 9 meant). But we knew that the water with gasoline needed more work.

We kept working—singing over and into the water, praying for the water, merging with the water, holding the water, and calling in all ancestral spirits who might know how to transmute it. At this point we felt the palpable presence of the spirits in the room. We also tried doing a shamanic extraction to take out illness from the water. We continued to work until we felt that we had done all we could.

The ammonium hydroxide water remained at a pH of 9. Woods tested that water kinesiologically and found that there was a significant positive change in it. I filled up the bottles in the test kit with the gasoline water and packed up the box to ship to the lab.

We closed our ceremony by holding hands and letting the spirits know that we were done for now. We released them and thanked them for all their help. Then we all shared food together.

The next day three of us reported feeling unusually depleted. We felt that we had become so goal-oriented and focused on the water that we just tried too hard to make something happen. We didn't find out until Sunday morning from Vic (the physicist) that we had made a significant change in the water with ammonium hydroxide and that we had turned poisonous water into water safe to drink. This helped to lift our spirits.

On Sunday we began our practice again with yoga and breathing. This helped to wake us up and clear our minds. The results of the yoga and breathing made us feel as if a fog had been lifted.

Our first journey was to get a critique from our helping spirits on the work we had done Saturday night. We were told that our work had gone well, and we were all reminded to keep working to get our egos out of the way. I was told that the gasoline was still as present in the water as before we started but that the water was beaming with light and life, meaning that we had been successful in changing the water to a state where the gasoline would not harm it. This gave me lots of food for thought, as I had never considered measuring the life force of the water.

The next journey we did was to ask to be dismembered and then transfigured. This was a very profound experience for the group members. I was also told at the end of my journey to stop transfiguring into the light, as I had been doing in my practice, but instead to transfigure into the void. The void, the blackness, is that state before creation begins, the place of unlimited possibilities, and the formlessness that all religious and spiritual traditions speak of. I have done a great deal of work with the void, and Isis is the teacher who has had me work in this place. In the journey she showed up and instructed me to become the void and let the light be created and shine through from this place. This was quite a profound teaching for me.

The group was so touched by the process of being transfigured into the divine that there were very few words to share, and I didn't want our talking to break the sacredness each person was feeling.

We ate, took a break, and separately spent time in nature. When we returned, we journeyed to get advice on how to bridge the dismemberment/transfiguration experience into our work that evening. We all received information that was important to us individually.

We ended our afternoon chanting songs from different traditions and began to prepare ourselves for the evening's work. On Saturday night I had dressed in ceremonial clothes and had worn certain objects I use for rituals. This night I decided to use the information in the dream I had had before going into the Great Pyramid about letting go of anything that weighed me down and prevented me from becoming divine energy. I wore simple clothes, including a shawl I always use in ceremony as a statement of respect to the spirits, and no jewelry.

We performed our ceremony in a similar way but with a few changes. We focused our intention not on changing the water, but rather on changing ourselves. We spent more time in the calling in of the spirits and singing and dancing in an effort to harmonize with the rhythm of nature and life. We did not do a separate ceremony to make the water holy, since from a divine place we recognized the water to be holy already. We used our power songs as well as the Sufi chant to help change our state of consciousness. We let go of the chants from other traditions, as they didn't take us as deeply into an ecstatic state. We did have a black mug filled with quinine water, and Kate, whose visual ability is strong, observed the deep blue color in the water. The deionized water we began with was at a pH of 5.5. We toned as Diana put the ammonium hydroxide into the water and I put in the gasoline. The purpose of the toning was to create a divine and holy state that would facilitate our process of transfiguration. Diana tested the pH of the adulterated water, which tonight was 12, and Woods tested all the water using kinesiology.

From a transfigured state we kept up the toning, and each of us worked with the water in our own way. When I picked up the bowls of water, I completely merged with them from a place of love, and I just rocked with them as we danced and sang together in the rhythm of life. I could hear all the toning and heard it as the song of the whole universe singing with us and through us. I had told the group that light drumming and rattling could be used to keep us in the transfigured state. None of us chose this option, and we just kept the toning going with no other sound. It was quite beautiful.

We finished in about twenty minutes, and then it was once again time to perform the testing. Woods, using kinesiology, said that all the water tested okay. The pH of the water with ammonium hydroxide had again gone down to 9. The quinine water had less blue in it, meaning that there was not so much quinine present.

We were in such an ecstatic state from the toning and transfiguration that we didn't want to end our work. We did another round of toning and transfiguring into the divine and healing the water.

When we stopped toning as a group, I could feel in a palpable way that the veils between the worlds had lifted and that the lines of communication with the spirits were open, strong, and clear. I suggested that we use healing words, as described in Part V, to pray for ourselves and the earth. We all sent out words to the universe that came from our heart.

We then thanked the spirits once again for their help and released them, letting them know that for now the work was done. I packed up the gasoline water into another test kit. We then had a great celebration and shared food, marking the end of our work of the weekend.

That night and the next day there was no sense of depletion; we were all recharged and filled with power.

On Saturday night, although we had been successful in transmuting the water with ammonium hydroxide, I felt that I had not changed. On Sunday, as we shifted from using divine intervention to embodying the divine, I felt I had now become a different person. Both nights the change in the water occurred in about fifteen to twenty minutes, which is quite extraordinary.

The important keys to the work, besides our focusing on the parts of the formula, was our forming a strong community and creating a partnership with the water, gasoline, ammonium hydroxide, and quinine, as well as all the time we spent creating a sacred space for the spirits to work in.

There was much that I learned from our work. I got the direct experience of how water is a living being. This understanding was beyond words for me, but it lived in all the cells of my body. I could now understand that when we dump pollutants into water, we are killing a living being. The same is true for all the other elements.

Perceiving the water we had made holy as not harmed by the

gasoline helped me to understand Jack Schwarz's experience of suffering no physiological trauma or pain from putting sailmaker's needles into his body. This was a great teaching in how we can neutralize harm from pollutants. At the same time, this ability doesn't give us the right to continue dumping pollutants in our environment. This, of course, raised an interesting question as far as the lab tests for the gasoline water. We have no tests to measure the life force of water and therefore have no scientific way to test whether the information I received from my helping spirits that the water was beaming and unharmed was true.

I also received the direct teaching that when we remember our divine nature, nature will reflect that back to us. I could experience the purity and the living being we call water being born as we worked on Sunday night.

The most direct change from our work that occurred for me was how I began perceiving the water I drink and use. I now see it as a living being, and I am in a greater place of appreciation of it in my life.

A month after our work I received the results from the lab for the bottles of water with gasoline. The results were inconclusive. The lab reports did show that there were differences between the various samples, but we could not figure out what pattern was occurring. When I spoke with Vic about this, he thought that the next time we should make up one batch of water mixed with gasoline and separate it out into different bottles. In this way, we would know we were working with the same amounts of gasoline.

As I shared our results with others, I was asked whether or not we had a control with the water with ammonium hydroxide. The concern was whether or not the pH would have changed on its own without any work. So I made a control batch and let it sit for two hours. The pH did not change.

The work we did created change for all of us. Gail shares some of what she learned:

I absolutely believe in miracles and that I can participate in the creation of a miracle. That one does not have to work hard but simply believe the spirits will do the work and give oneself over to helping them in whatever way one can. I learned that each of us was needed, for we each held an important piece. I have learned the importance of humility. I felt our group was humble and thus the spirits knew of our sweet and honest intention. I learned that I must work on my own humility in all aspects of my daily life.

She continues with how she has changed from the experience:

I am more open, more spacious. The openness has to do with being a "hollow bone," but also I feel a new and greater openness to others and the world. When I returned I was able to consciously see and feel the fear that my old self and ego had of the new changes. I put the circle's wishes over my own. I am not sure I have ever felt that giving up of selfishness that strongly ever before. I feel so much softer. I do not feel as time-bound.

Diana shares:

I've learned that to even approach this work of transmutation and transfiguration requires the total willingness and ability to surrender to source, Allah, god, goddess. We can make a request, send our prayers, but must ultimately concentrate on "Thy will be done."

This work requires consciously being what we are—a part of the grand web of creation, the movement and manifestation of the divine.

I sense a different vulnerability and power, expansiveness and longing. I continue to experience a certain kind of streaming, bright energy that heightens all senses as one, makes me very aware of any blocks, and brings deep wonder and gratitude.

The experience of grace, oneness, and light that can come from surrender of the "little self" can certainly bring joy and bliss. I know I am still human and my ego is alive and well. Yet I also know that I have opened to spirit more than ever before and will never be the same.

I now understand more deeply that this work is best done in a group. We need each other as mirrors and focusers. Group work also keeps us from taking any ego credit or blame as individuals for what happens or doesn't happen. And together we receive an immediate and concrete experience of seeking union in the circle and then reaching out to the whole web of life.

We decided to see if the work would also be successful with long-distance healing. We decided that I should make up the water with ammonium hydroxide and Diana, Gail, and Kate would work on it from Colorado. I had told Gail that the water would be on my kitchen counter. At the last minute I decided to make up another bowl and put it in my living room. Only I knew it was there.

The three woman journeyed and came up with a ceremony to use. Ceremonies that are performed as a recipe have no power, so they used a ceremony similar to the one we had done together but made it their own. They used their own words to invoke the spirits, and they did more singing, dancing, and drumming.

They called me when they were done, and I tested the water. The pH of the water in the kitchen had changed from 11 to 9.5, but there was no change in the control in my living room.

One month later we tried a third experiment in which Vic made up the water with ammonium hydroxide at his and Diana's home in Colorado. I was leading a two-week workshop on shamanic practices with a group of seventy-five people. On our last night together we attempted to change the pH of the water Vic made up. None of us had been to Diana or Vic's house; we only had an address to go on.

We spent the day in preparation, merging with water and doing a dismemberment/transfiguration journey. We called in the spirits, danced and sang, and worked in the same way the other group had in January with transfiguring into the divine or the helping spirits. This time we focused on the water at the address given to us.

Vic had made up the water two hours before to test if the water would change on its own—it didn't. After about thirty minutes of working, the pH had changed from 11 to 10. Although the results were not as dramatic as when the water was in our presence, they were significant. Vic said there is no scientific explanation for this change.

After we were done I surveyed the group to find out how people had worked. Five people had not used transfiguration and had only asked for divine intervention. Of the rest of the group, half had used only transfiguration and the other half had used both transfiguration and asking for divine intervention.

As I received letters from the workshop participants in the following weeks I was touched by how much positive change had manifested in their lives.

Diana, Gail, Kate, Woods, and I have continued our long-distance experimentation, with Vic making up the water. Vic has tried different controls, such as testing the pH of the water for many hours before and after.

In our most recent long-distance work, the pH changed from 11.5 to 10 in thirty minutes. This indicates that even with all of us working from different locations our work changed the nature of the water by 30 percent.

There is much more experimentation to do, and I am excited about continuing my work with this. At some point I envision moving away from working with a bowl of water and taking this knowledge of transmutation to our polluted water sources. I also look forward to working with all the elements, not just water.

As I mentioned many times, it is not just the ceremonies we perform that will make the difference. It is who we become that is the true medicine for the earth.

Appendix

Here is a simple exercise to work with to help you when mental chatter stands in the way of being able to see, hear, feel, smell, or taste what your intuition is expressing.

Sit down, close your eyes, and take three deep breaths.

Think about something you love—a smell, a taste, a feeling, a sensation, a sound, or a color.

Experience fully this thing you are telling yourself you love. Say, "I love _____."

Notice the cues you receive when you tell yourself a truth. Do you see an image? Do you feel relaxed and warm? Do you hear a sound? Do you smell or taste something?

Now get up and walk around for a few minutes to clear your experience. You might try doing a menial task. After a few minutes sit down, close your eyes, and take three deep breaths.

Tell yourself that you hate what you just told yourself you loved—meaning tell yourself a lie.

Notice the cues your body give you when you hear a lie. Is there an image? What do you see, feel, hear, smell, or taste?

When I hear a truth, I see the green light on a traffic signal shining. When my intuition is saying no or stop, or telling me that something is a lie, I feel a tight sensation in my solar plexus, and I see the bright red light from a traffic signal.

Using your body cues will interpret what your intuition is telling you.

Training Workshops

To stay informed about the transmutation work being done by Sandra Ingerman, and to receive a schedule of workshops taught by Sandra on transmutation and/or shamanic methods, please write to:

Sandra Ingerman
P.O. Box 4757
Santa Fe, New Mexico 87502

You can also visit my Web site for news on my work with transmutation: www.shamanicvisions.com/ingerman.html.

For information on how to join in on monthly meditations for the purpose of forming a web of light for global healing, please write me or visit my Web site.

Notes

○ INTRODUCTION

1. Eliade, *Shamanism: Archaic Techniques,* 5.
2. Cox, *Pillar of Celestial Fire,* 255.
3. Hall, *Secret Teachings,* LII.
4. Ibid., LXVIII.
5. Metzner, *Unfolding Self,* 14.
6. Hall, *Secret Teachings,* CLVI.
7. Ibid., CL–CLI.
8. Roth with Occhiogrosso, *Healing Path of Prayer,* 90.
9. Somé, *Ritual,* 17–18.
10. Prophet, *St. Germain,* 6.
11. Casey, *Making the Gods Work,* 8.

I CREATION AND UNION

○ 1 THE CREATION MYTH

1. Roth with Occhiogrosso, *Healing Path of Prayer,* 72.
2. Schwarz, *How to Master the Art of Personal Health,* 4.
3. Ibid., 19–21.
4. Hislop, *My Baba,* 132.
5. Sproul, *Primal Myths,* 14.
6. Ibid., 16–17.
7. Roth with Occhiogrosso, *Healing Path of Prayer,* 68–69.
8. Ibid., 29.
9. Houston, *The Passion of Isis and Osiris,* 28.
10. Ibid., 28–30.
11. Ellis, *Awakening of Osiris,* 19–21.
12. This myth was adapted from Reed, *Aboriginal Myth,* 19–21.

O 2 T O O L S T O E M B O D Y Y O U R C R E A T I O N S T O R Y

1. Fortune, *Mystical Qabalah*, 29.
2. Sproul, *Primal Myths*, 14.
3. Hislop, *My Baba*, 105.
4. Bachofen, *Myth, Religion, and Mother Right*, 49.
5. Gass with Brehoney, *Chanting*, 16.
6. Lidell with N. and G. Rabinovitch, *Sivananda Companion to Yoga*, 98.
7. Gass with Brehoney, *Chanting*, 12.
8. Ingerman, *Fall to Grace*, 115–16.

II SEPARATION VERSUS UNION

O 3 R E M E M B E R I N G O U R C O N N E C T I O N

1. Roth with Occhiogrosso, *Healing Path of Prayer*, 172–73.
2. Gass with Brehoney, *Chanting*, 53.

O 4 R E M E M B E R I N G T H E B E A U T Y

1. Ingerman, *Fall to Grace*, 136.
2. West, *Serpent in the Sky*, 123.
3. Rike, unpublished sermon, 1999. Jennifer Rike is a minister and teaches
   theology at the University of Detroit, Detroit, Michigan.
4. Schwarz, *How to Master the Art of Personal Health*, 5–6.
5. Ibid., 12.
6. Ibid., 22–23.
7. Ibid., 29–31.
8. Frankl, *Man's Search*, 126.

O 5 W H E N T H I N G S F E E L B A D

1. Schwarz, *How to Master the Art of Personal Health*, 23–25.
2. Narayan, *River Joins the Ocean*, 19–20.
3. Maharshi, *Be as You Are*, 65.
4. Assagioli, *Act of Will*, 213–17. This exercise was taught to me in a
   psychosynthesis class in 1979. It is an adaptation from the exercise in *Act
   of Will*.

○ 6 M O R E T O O L S T O H E L P

1. Ingerman, *Fall to Grace*, 91.
2. Wilhelm/Baynes, *I Ching*. This teaching appears throughout the book.

III LOVE AND IMAGINATION

○ 7 C R E A T I N G S A C R E D S P A C E

1. This story of Isis and Osiris is adapted from *The Search for Omm Sety*, 65.

○ 8 I M A G I N A T I O N

1. Dossey, *Meaning and Medicine*, 227.
2. Crichton, *Sphere*, 335.
3. Page, as quoted by Morgan, *Cassadaga*, 187.
4. Neville, *Law*, 89.
5. Ibid., 103.
6. Ibid., 113.
7. Ibid., 135.
8. Ibid., 140.
9. Casey, *Making the Gods Work*, 14.
10. Houston, *Passion of Isis and Osiris*, 193.
11. Browning, Paracelsus 13, cited in Neville, *Seedtime*, 116.
12. Ingerman, *Welcome Home*, 17.
13. Casey, *Making the Gods Work*, 14.

○ 9 R E C E I V I N G T H E G I F T S O F O U R A N C E S T O R S

1. Houston, *Passion of Isis and Osiris*, 224.

IV HARMONY WITH NATURE WITHIN AND WITHOUT

○ 10 R E C O N N E C T I N G W I T H N A T U R E

1. Dossey, *Be Careful What You Pray For*, 216–17. He reprinted this from
   Richard Wilhelm, *The Secret of the Golden Flower: A Chinese Book of Life*,
   trans. Cary F. Baynes, rev. ed. (New York: Harvest/HBJ, 1962). The story
   was told in *Jung: His Life and Work* (Boston: Shambhala, 1991), 128.
2. Moss and Corbin, "Shamanism and the Spirits of Weather," quoted in
   Swan, *Nature as Healer*, 4.
3. Ingerman, *Soul Retrieval*, 194.

○ 11 Working with Cycles and Rhythms in Nature

1. Hall, *Secret Teachings,* LI.
2. Casey, *Making the Gods Work,* 265.
3. Knight-Ridder Newspapers, reprinted in *The New Mexican,* Santa Fe, NM, 17 August 1999.

○ 13 A Shift of Perception

1. Casey, *Making the Gods Work,* 11.

V TRANSMUTATION

○ 15 Dismemberment

1. Metzner, *Unfolding Self,* 101–2.
2. Larson, *Shaman's Doorway,* 63.
3. Thurman, *Hidden Truths,* 226–27.
4. Frawley, *Tantric Yoga,* 67–68.
5. Hall, *Secret Teachings,* CLVI.
6. Ibid., CLXX.
7. Benson, *Relaxation Response,* 133–34.

○ 16 Transfiguration

1. Roth with Occhiogrosso, *Healing Path of Prayer,* 197–98.
2. Metzner, *Unfolding Self,* 162, quoting from Lama Govinda's *Foundation of Tibetan Mysticism,* 164.
3. Blau, *Krishnamurti,* 173–75.
4. Peters, "Mystical Experience in Tamang Shamanism," *Revision* 13, 2 (1990): 79.
5. Metzner, *Unfolding Self,* 164.
6. Murphet, *Sai Baba,* 59–65.

○ 17 The Power of Sound and Words

1. Gass with Brehoney, *Chanting,* 58.
2. Ibid., 43.
3. Reid, *Harnessing,* 144.

4. Gass with Brehoney, *Chanting,* 36.

5. The Hindu story of creation from Kali's necklace comes from Houston, *Passion of Isis and Osiris,* 182.

6. Wasserman, *Egyptian Book of the Dead,* 145.

7. Houston, *Passion of Isis and Osiris,* 182; this is from an excerpt from Erik Hornung, *Conceptions of God in Ancient Egypt* (Ithaca, NY: Cornell University Press, 1982), 175.

8. Casey, *Making the Gods Work,* 216.

19 MORE TO THINK ABOUT

1. Neville, *Seedtime,* 141–42.

VI CEREMONIES FOR TRANSMUTATION

20 THE NATURE OF CEREMONIES

1. Somé, *Ritual,* 32–33.

2. Ibid., 24.

3. Houston, *Passion of Isis and Osiris,* 192.

4. Casey, *Making the Gods Work,* 83.

23 CEREMONIES FOR WORKING IN PARTNERSHIP

1. Yont, "Disaster in the Amazon: Brazil Indians Call Spirits to Fight Fires," *Philadelphia Inquirer,* 8 April 1998, reprinted from World Wide Web.

Bibliography

Andreas, Brian. *Still Mostly True.* Iowa: StoryPeople, 1994.

Argüelles, José, and Miriam Argüelles. *Mandala.* Boston: Shambhala, 1995.

Assagioli, Roberto. *The Act of Will.* New York: Penguin Books, 1976.

Bachofen, J. J. *Myth, Religion, and Mother Right.* Trans. Ralph Manheim. Bollingen Series, vol. 84. Princeton, NJ: Princeton University Press, 1967.

Benson, Herbert, M.D. *The Relaxation Response.* New York: Avon Books, 1976.

Blau, Evelyne. *Krishnamurti, 100 Years.* New York: Stewart, Tabori, and Chang, 1995.

Budge, Sir Wallace. *Egyptian Magic.* Secaucus, NJ: Carol, 1997.

———. *Egyptian Religion.* Secaucus, NJ: Carol, 1997.

Campbell, Don. *The Mozart Effect.* New York: Avon, 1997.

Casey, Caroline W. *Making the Gods Work for You.* New York: Three Rivers, 1998.

Cassadaga: The South's Spiritualist Community. Edited by John J. Guthrie Jr., Phillip C. Lucas, and Gary Monroe. Gainesville: University Press of Florida, 2000.

The Catholic Encyclopedia. First published by the Encyclopedia Press, 1913. New Advent Electronic Version, copyright 1996.

Cott, Jonathan, with Hanny El Zeini. *The Search for Omm Sety.* London: Random House, 1992.

Cox, Robert. *The Pillar of Celestial Fire and the Lost Service of the Ancient Seers.* Fairfield, IA: Sunstar, 1997.

Crichton, Michael. *Sphere.* New York: Ballantine Books, 1988.

DeBecker, Gavin. *The Gift of Fear: Survival Signals that Protect Us from Violence.* Boston: Little Brown, 1997.

Dossey, Larry, M.D. *Be Careful What You Pray For . . . You Just Might Get It.* San Francisco: HarperSanFrancisco, 1997.

———. *Meaning and Medicine: A Doctor's Tale of Breakthrough and Healing.* New York: Bantam, 1991.

Eliade, Mircea. *Shamanism: Archaic Techniques of Ecstasy.* Trans. Willard R. Trask. Bollingen Series, vol. 76. Princeton, NJ: Princeton University Press, 1972.

Ellis, Normandi. *Awakening Osiris: The Egyptian Book of the Dead.* Grand Rapids, MI: Phanes, 1988.

Fortune, Dion. *The Mystical Qabalah.* York Beach, ME: Samuel Weiser, 1997.

Frankl, Victor E. *Man's Search for Meaning.* New York: Washington Square, 1985.

Frawley, David. *Tantric Yoga and the Wisdom Goddesses: Spiritual Secrets of Ayurveda.* Salt Lake City: Passage, 1994.

Gass, Robert, with Kathleen Brehony. *Chanting: Discovering Spirit in Sound.* New York: Broadway, 1999.

Grant, Joan. *Winged Pharaoh.* Alpharetta, GA: Ariel, 1985.

Hall, Manly P. *The Secret Teachings of All Ages.* Los Angeles: Philosophical Research Society, 1977.

Harding, Elizabeth U. *Kali: The Black Goddess of Dakshineswar.* York Beach, ME: Nicholas-Hays, 1993.

Harner, Michael. *The Way of the Shaman.* 3rd ed. San Francisco: Harper and Row, 1990 (originally published in 1980).

Hidden Truths: Magic, Alchemy, and the Occult. Ed. Lawrence E. Sullivan from *Religion, History and Culture: Selections from: The Encyclopedia of Religion.* Editor in chief, Mircea Eliade, New York: Macmillan, 1989.

Hislop, John S. *My Baba and I.* San Diego: Birth Day, 1985.

Hornung, Erik. *Conceptions of God in Ancient Egypt.* Ithaca, New York: Cornell University Press, 1982.

Houston, Jean. *The Passion of Isis and Osiris: A Union of Two Souls.* New York: Ballantine, 1995.

The I Ching or Book of Changes. Trans. Richard Wilhelm, rendered into English by Cary F. Baynes. Bollingen Series, vol. 19. Princeton, NJ: Princeton University Press, 1950.

Ingerman, Sandra. *A Fall to Grace.* Santa Fe, NM: Moon Tree Rising Productions, 1997.

———. *Welcome Home: Following Your Soul's Journey Home.* San Francisco: HarperSanFrancisco, 1994.

———. *Soul Retrieval: Mending the Fragmented Self.* San Francisco: HarperSanFrancisco, 1991.

Keys, David. *Catastrophe: A Quest for the Origins of the Modern World.* New York: Ballantine, 2000.

Kohn, Livia, with Yoshinabu Sakade, eds. and trans. *Taoist Meditation and Longevity Techniques.* Ann Arbor, MI: University of Michigan Center for Chinese Studies, 1989.

Larsen, Stephen. *The Shaman's Doorway.* Berrytown, NY: Station Hill, 1988.

Lidell, Lucy, with Narayani Rabinovitch and Giris Rabinovitch. *The Sivananda Companion to Yoga.* New York: Simon and Schuster, 1983.

Maharshi, Sri Ramana. *Be as You Are: The Teachings of Sri Ramana Maharshi.* Ed. David Godman. London, Boston, Melbourne, Henley: Arkana, 1985.

Markides, Kyriacos C. *Fire in the Heart.* New York: Arkana, 1991.

Metzner, Ralph. *The Unfolding Self: Varieties of Transformative Experiences.* Novato: Origin Press, 1986, 1998.

Moss, Nan, and David Corbin. "Shamanism and the Spirits of Weather: More Pieces of the Puzzle." *Shamanism,* 2, 2 (1999). Fall/Winter 1999.

Murphet, Howard. *Sai Baba Avatar: A New Journey into Power and Glory.* San Diego: Birth Day, 1977.

Narayan, G. *As the River Joins the Ocean: Reflections About J. Krishnamurti.* India: Book Faith, 1998.

Neville. *Awakened Imagination, Including the Search.* Marina del Rey, CA: DeVorss, 1992.

———. *Seedtime and Harvest.* Marina del Rey, CA: DeVorsss, 1992.

———. *the Law and the Promise.* Marina del Rey, CA: DeVorss, 1992.

———. *The Power of Awareness.* Ed. Victoria Goddard. Rev. ed. Marina del Rey, CA: DeVorss, 1992.

Ornstein, Robert, and David Sobel, M.D. *Healthy Pleasure.* Reading, MA: Perseus Books, 1998.

Peters, Larry. "Mystical Experience in Tamang Shamanism." *Trance, Initiation, and Psychotherapy in Nepalese Shamanism: Essays on Tamang and Tibetan Shamanism.*

———. "Shamanism: Phenomenology of a Spiritual Discipline," *Trance, Initiation, and Psychotherapy in Nepalese Shamanism: Essays on Tamang and Tibetan Shamanism.* First published in *The Journal of Transpersonal Psychology,* 1989, vol. 21, no. 2.

Prophet, Elizabeth Clare. *St. Germain on Alchemy: Formulas for Self-Transformations.* Recorded by Mark L. Prophet. Livingston, MT: Summit University Press, 1995.

Reed, A.W. *Aboriginal Myth: Tales of the Dreamtime.* Reed Books Pty. Ltd. Terrey Hills, N.S.W., 1978.

Reid, Daniel. *Harnessing the Power of the Universe.* Boston and London: Shambhala, 1998.

Roth, Ron, with Peter Occhiogrosso. *The Healing Path of Prayer: A Modern Mystic's Guide to Spiritual Power.* New York: Three Rivers, 1997.

Schwarz, Jack. *How to Master the Art of Personal Health: The Power of Attaining and Maintaining Your Health.* Grants Pass, OR: Schwarz, 1996.

Seven Taoist Masters: A Folk Novel of China. Trans. Eva Wong. Boston: Shambhala, 1990.

Somé, Malidoma Patrice. *Ritual, Power Healing, and Community.* New York: Penguin/Arkana, 1997.

Sproul, Barbara C. *Primal Myths: Creation Myths Around the World.* San Francisco: HarperSanFrancisco, 1991.

Wasserman, James. *The Egyptian Book of the Dead: The Book of Going Forth by Day.* Trans. Raymond Faulkner. San Francisco, CA: Chronicle Books, 1994.

West, John Anthony. *Serpent in the Sky: The High Wisdom of Ancient Egypt.* 2nd ed. Wheaton, IL: Quest, 1993.

Woodman, Marion, and Elinor Dickson. *Dancing in the Flames: The Dark Goddess in the Transformation of Consciousness.* Boston: Shambhala, 1997.

Wright, Machaelle Small. *Behaving as if the God in All Life Mattered.* Jeffersonton, VA: Perelandra, 1987.

Acknowledgments

I give thanks to:

Barbara Moulton, my agent, and Patricia Gift, my editor at Crown Publishers, for believing in me and my work.

Woods Shoemaker for his love and support throughout all the stages of this work, and for helping me pioneer the work of transmutation.

Brooke London Isberg for her endless support and help with research and typing.

Gail Mesplay for her help in research.

Diana Guth, Kate Jones, and Gail Mesplay for their willingness to pioneer through journeywork and experimentation the work of transmutation with me.

Katherine Hubbard for her friendship and the light and inspiration she shared with me through her illness and her death.

Janice Springer for helping me research biblical stories.

Troy Cucchiara and Greg Friedman at the Good Water Company in Santa Fe for their support, patience, and guidance in helping me come up with ideas of pollutants to work with in water for the purpose of experimenting with ceremonies for transmutation.

Vic Petrovsky for sharing his expertise and devising an experiment with water in which we could test our results as we were working. His work was truly invaluable to us.

Jennifer Rike for allowing me to share her sermon.

Barbara Moulton for her generosity in helping me with editing and the format.

Kieran O'Brien at Crown Publishers for all her help and patience.

Tim Roethgen at Crown Publishers for his help with publicity.

Ellen Kleiner, Ann Mason, and Heidi Utz for their assistance in editing.

Jeanne Achterberg for her encouragement and guidance.

Michael Harner and Angeles Arrien, the teachers who started me off on my path leading into this work.

My parents, Aaron and Lee Ingerman, for their unconditional love and support of me as a person.

The participants of the 2000 two-week intensive course in advanced shamanism and shamanic healing and the fourth East Coast three-year program for their support and participation in the work.

StoryPeople, www.storypeople.com.

My ancestors, who passed down their gifts and strengths to me.

My power animals, teachers, and all the gods and goddesses of Egypt who have been so generous with the love and teachings that have allowed me to call and bring forth this book and work.

The spirits of the land and spring where I live, who created the sacred space in which I could write.

The spirit of Santa Fe for all her teachings.

Index

shadow, 51, 52
Shamanism: Archaic Techniques of Ecstasy (Eliade), 2, 177
shamans, shamanism, 1–3, 27, 38, 39, 52, 60, 103–4, 108, 112, 154, 180, 190, 191, 196, 203, 230, 247, 249
Shiva, 15, 174
Somé, Malidoma, 9, 224
songs, singing, 37, 38–39, 40–41, 42, 43, 44, 154, 226, 243, 251
  composing, 41
  power, 37, 38–39, 41
  using, 41–42
soul, 55, 58–65
  remembering true nature of, 58–65
  spirit vs., 58–59
soul loss, 59–60, 108
soul retrieval, 59–60, 107–8
Soul Retrieval: Mending the Fragmented Self (Ingerman), 13, 59, 136, 157–58
sound, power of, 201–5, 249
Sphere (Crichton), 109–10
spirit, 28
  connection with, 49–50, 51–56, 131
  soul vs., 58–59
  tools for remembering connection with, 54–55
spirits, 28
  helping, 27–28, 241, 252
  of nature, working with, 157–61, 237–38, 239–40
spiritual side, 51, 52–53
Sproul, Barbara, 21, 23, 35
stars, 67
stress, 132, 140
sun, 28, 140, 141, 143–44, 145, 147, 149, 152, 251
symbols, 35–37, 43, 44, 65

Tantric Yoga and the Wisdom Goddesses (Frawley), 180
teachers, 123–24
Thich Nhat Hanh, 55
thoughts, 112, 203, 204
  observing, 82
thoughts, negative, 75, 76
  releasing, 230–31
  transmutation of, 244–45
Thurman, Robert, 180
thyroid, 132
toning, 41, 243

tragedy, 116
transfiguration, 189–99, 243
transformation and healing, ceremonies for, 243–50
transmutation, 4, 5–6, 7–8, 11–12, 13–14, 15, 16, 167–217
  appreciation and gratefulness and, 207–11
  ceremonies for, *see* ceremonies for transmutation
  dismemberment and, 177–87, 191, 192–93, 194, 196–97
  and embodying the divine, 169–75
  of energy in a space, 246–47
  failure of, 214–17
  of food, 245–46
  formula for, 12–13, 47, 72–73, 86–87, 95–96, 106, 118–19, 125–26, 165–66, 198–99, 205, 210–11, 254, 255
  of negative energy and emotions, 76–80, 84, 244–45
  by perceiving all energy as neutral, 247–48
  sound and words in, 201–5, 249
  transfiguration and, 189–99, 243
  of water, 153, 168, 183, 248–50, 257–69
tree, merging with, 128–29
Trismosin, Solomon, 8

The Unfolding Self (Metzner), 7, 179, 190, 191
union, 204
  embodying vs., 170
  in formula for transmutation, 12, 47, 73, 86, 95, 106, 118, 125, 165, 199, 205, 211, 254

walking in nature, 64, 153–54
water, 28, 149–50, 151, 152, 153, 154, 155, 160
  transmutation of, 153, 168, 183, 248–50, 257–69
weather, 160, 237–38, 239–40, 241
Welcome Home: Following Your Soul's Journey Home (Ingerman), 13, 60, 66, 115–16, 192
West, John Anthony, 63
Wilhelm, Richard, 134
words, power of, 201–5, 249
workplaces, 23

About the Author

SANDRA INGERMAN is the author of *Soul Retrieval: Mending the Fragmented Self* (Harper San Francisco, 1991), *Welcome Home: Following Your Soul's Journey Home* (Harper San Francisco, 1993), and *A Fall to Grace* (Moon Tree Rising Productions, 1997). She has also recorded a two-tape three-hour lecture, "The Soul Retrieval Journey" (Sounds True, 1997). She is the leading practitioner of soul retrieval and is the former educational director of The Foundation for Shamanic Studies. Sandra has a master's in counseling psychology from the California Institute of Integral Studies and teaches workshops on shamanism around the world. She is recognized for bridging the ancient cross-cultural healing methods into our modern culture, addressing the needs of our times. Sandra is a licensed marriage and family therapist and professional mental health counselor in the state of New Mexico.

To receive a calendar of international workshops on shamanism and a schedule of workshops on transmutation, please write the author at:

P.O. Box 4757
Santa Fe, New Mexico 87502